Get Se
Go

I0069225

Go programming fundamentals,
environment setup, and core concepts

Amrit Pal Singh

www.bpbonline.com

First Edition 2025

Copyright © BPB Publications, India

ISBN: 978-93-65898-866

To View Complete
BPB Publications Catalogue
Scan the QR Code:

www.bpbonline.com

Dedicated to

*My wife, **Dilraj**, and my daughter, **Jesmyra***

About the Author

Amrit Pal Singh is currently serving as Sr. Director of Cloud Software at Jubilee TV, based in Bengaluru, India. With a career spanning over 20 years, he has extensive experience in various domains. These include high-performance web backend platforms, cloud services deployment, media middleware, and firmware development.

Amrit holds a master's degree in software systems from Birla Institute of Technology and Science, Pilani. He has authored patents in the field of media content management.

In addition to his technical roles, Amrit is an active content creator on YouTube, where he shares insights on technology and software programming. His areas of interest include product development, system software and firmware, web-scale cloud computing system architectures, and ML and AI.

About the Reviewers

❖ **Shrinath Thube** is a seasoned software developer at IBM, USA, and a technology leader with extensive experience in cloud, cybersecurity, observability, and AI-driven automation. He specializes in building scalable and secure solutions, driving innovations in IBM Cloud, **application performance monitoring (APM)**, and enterprise security. His expertise spans microservices architecture, governance and compliance, container security, and AI-powered automation.

With a strong track record of leading mission-critical projects, Shrinath has enhanced system reliability, integrated security frameworks, and optimized cloud-based solutions for improved performance and visibility. He has worked extensively with modern cloud technologies, including Kubernetes, OpenShift, and security, ensuring seamless and secure deployments.

Beyond technical contributions, Shrinath is passionate about mentoring, cross-functional collaboration, and driving innovation in emerging technologies. As a Technology Advisory Board Member at Avotrix, he provides strategic insights on AI adoption, cloud security, and observability, helping organizations navigate technological advancements and strengthen their security posture. He also serves as an Industry Expert on the Board of Studies for multiple academic institutions, shaping curriculum development and bridging the gap between education and industry needs.

Shaped by a strong academic foundation, Shrinath holds a master's degree in electrical engineering from San Jose State University, USA. He is an active Senior IEEE Member and IEEE Computer Society Member, contributing to the global technology community through thought leadership, technical publications, and industry collaborations. Committed to bridging research and real-world applications, he continues to leverage technology to build secure, scalable, and intelligent solutions that drive business success.

❖ **Vishwa** is passionate about writing clean, efficient, and maintainable code and is a strong advocate for best practices in software engineering, including **test-driven development (TDD)**, code reviews, and continuous improvement.

Currently, Vishwa is working at Publicis Sapient , where he is leading the development of cutting-edge microservices solutions that drive business value and innovation.

Vishwa, thrives on solving complex technical challenges and enjoys mentoring teams to elevate their skills in Go and distributed systems. He is committed to helping organizations harness the full potential of Golang to build scalable, reliable, and high-performance applications.

Acknowledgement

I would like to express my sincere gratitude to everyone who contributed to this book. A special thanks to my family and friends for their unwavering support and encouragement. Your love and motivation have been invaluable.

I am very grateful to BPB Publications for their guidance and expertise in bringing this book to life. Their support was crucial in navigating the publishing process. Thank you to the reviewers, technical experts, and editors for your valuable feedback. Your insights have greatly improved the quality of the book.

Finally, I want to thank the readers for your interest and support. Thank you to everyone who helped make this book a reality.

Preface

Go (Golang) is vital in today's software development and is a modern and efficient language. The book covers essential concepts for Go programming.

This book has thirteen focused chapters. It covers topics for understanding Go. We start with an introduction to Go and its setup. This guides you through setting up your environment. We then cover data types and control structures. Functions and error handling are also explained. Working with strings and slices builds a solid base. You will learn Go's core syntax and features.

Chapters 5 through 7 explore advanced topics. These include Go reflections and concurrency. Structs, methods, and interfaces are also covered. These showcase Go's unique capabilities. You will learn to build concurrent applications. Working with JSON and HTTP is discussed. Logging and testing are also covered. The usage of Go for web development and distributed systems is explained. These show how Go creates real-world solutions. Finally, we cover generics. An overview of Go for security and cryptography is also included. You will learn about advancements and secure coding.

This book is for anyone learning Go. It is for beginners and experienced developers. It is a portable reference and a guide to Go's key concepts for students and professionals.

Get Set Go aims to equip readers with knowledge. You will learn to write clean, efficient and maintainable Go code. You can build web servers, command-line tools, and distributed systems with this knowledge. I hope this book is a valuable resource. It will help you explore Go programming.

Chapter 1: Introduction to Go - This chapter dives into the fundamentals of Go and explore the historical context behind its creation. It starts by uncovering the reasons that led to the development of the language and examines how its design addresses the challenges of large-scale software engineering. Key milestones in Go's evolution are highlighted, showcasing why it has become a go-to choice for modern software solutions. Along the way, we will examine the features that set Go apart, such as simplicity, efficiency, and effectiveness in building scalable and high-performance applications. Additionally, the chapter introduces the essential fmt package, demonstrating how it can be used to format and print output effectively.

Chapter 2: Data Types and Control Structures - In this chapter, we will explore the core building blocks of Go, data types and control structures. We will cover Go's basic types—integers, floats, strings, and booleans—and the concept of zero values. Zero values are default values assigned to uninitialized variables.

We will also dive into variable declaration methods using var, type inference, shorthand declarations, and variable scope. Composite types like arrays, slices, maps, and structs are explained, along with constants and enumerations using iota.

You will learn to manage program flow with conditional statements and looping constructs. Finally, we will address type conversions in Go's statically typed system. By the end, you will be well-versed in handling data and controlling program execution in Go.

Chapter 3: Functions and Error Handling - In Go, functions are a fundamental component of building any application. They enable code reusability, modularity, and organization. Understanding how to declare and use functions is key to writing clean and maintainable code. This chapter covers the syntax for declaring functions, different types of parameters, and return values. It also touches upon advanced concepts like variadic functions, anonymous functions, closures, and error handling. By mastering these topics, you will be equipped to write more flexible and reliable code in Go.

We will also dive into error handling topics like throwing errors, defining, and handling custom errors.

Chapter 4: Strings and Files - In this chapter, we will delve into two fundamental aspects of programming in Go: string manipulation and file handling. This chapter explores Go's built-in packages, the strings and os packages. We will discuss essential string manipulation functions, UTF-8 encoding, and immutable string behavior. Additionally, we will dive into file and directory handling, which is essential for managing data storage, creating files and directories, and handling input and output operations. Command line arguments will also be covered. It gives us the flexibility to interact with programs directly from the terminal. Together, these topics provide a strong foundation for building powerful applications in Go.

Chapter 5: Go Reflection - Reflection in Go is a powerful feature that allows developers to inspect and manipulate types and values at runtime. This capability can make your code more dynamic and flexible. It enables you to write programs that can adapt to different types and structures without knowing them at compile time. In this chapter, we will explore the fundamentals of Go's reflect package, which provides the tools necessary for reflection. We will cover how to extract type information, work with values, and even modify them programmatically.

Chapter 6: Concurrency - Concurrency is one of Go's most powerful features that lets us write programs that are efficient at performing multiple tasks simultaneously. Concurrency in Go is driven by the lightweight and highly efficient nature of goroutines. In this chapter, we will delve into Go's concurrency model, exploring goroutines, channels, and synchronization mechanisms. Additionally, we will also explore the context package and understand how this package helps manage goroutines.

Chapter 7: Structs, Methods, and Interfaces - Structs are a foundational feature in Go that allow developers to group related data into cohesive units. Unlike arrays and slices, which store elements of a single type, structs can hold fields of differing types. In this chapter, we will explore how to define, instantiate, and use structs in Go. We will delve into advanced features like struct embedding for creating composite structures, overriding embedded fields, and defining methods to attach behavior to structs, enabling more organized and maintainable code. We will also cover interfaces, their implementation, type assertion and type switch statement.

Chapter 8: Working with JSON and HTTP - In modern web development, handling data efficiently and building robust HTTP servers are fundamental skills. Go's standard library provides powerful tools to achieve this. The net/http package creates web servers and the encoding/json package seamlessly works with JSON data. This chapter dives into these essential components, offering a comprehensive guide to building web applications in Go. From encoding and decoding JSON to implementing middleware and context handling, you will learn how to create efficient, and maintainable web servers that cater to dynamic client requirements.

Chapter 9: Logging and Testing - In the world of software development, logging and testing are indispensable tools that ensure the reliability and maintainability of applications. Logging provides insights into the behavior of a program, helping developers diagnose issues and understand application flow. Testing, on the other hand, verifies that code behaves as expected, preventing bugs and regressions.

In this chapter, we will explore the logging capabilities provided by Go, including the use of the log package and the newer slog package for structured logging. We will also delve into Go's testing framework, covering how to write unit tests, run benchmarks, and effectively debug your code.

Chapter 10: Go in Web Development - Web development with Go has gained traction due to its simplicity, performance, and concurrency support. Unlike many other languages, Go offers a robust standard library with built-in packages like net/http for web servers and html/template for rendering dynamic content. This reduces the need for external dependencies. Go's strong typing and compile-time checks help catch errors early. The lightweight goroutines enable efficient handling of thousands of concurrent requests. Additionally, Go's cross-compilation support ensures seamless deployment across platforms.

In this chapter, we will explore how to build web applications using Go, covering essential concepts such as building a simple web server, templating, handling forms and user input, integrating with popular web frameworks, and implementing basic authentication and session management.

Chapter 11: Go in Distributed Systems - In modern software development, distributed systems have become a cornerstone for building scalable and resilient applications. Go, with its simplicity and efficiency, is well-suited for developing such systems. This chapter delves into the use of Go in distributed systems, focusing on microservices, the context packages, and integrating with Apache Kafka using the Sarama library. We will also explore implementing distributed locks using Redis.

Chapter 12: Generics - In this chapter, we will explore one of Go's most anticipated features—generics. Generics were introduced in Go 1.18. Generics enable us to write reusable and flexible code by making functions and data structures to work with any data type while maintaining type safety. This chapter provides a guide to the syntax and structure of generics, from simple type parameters to advanced constraints. You will learn how to create generic functions and types, and use constraints to restrict type parameters.

Chapter 13: Go for Security and Cryptography - Security is a crucial aspect of software development, and Go provides robust tools to help developers secure their applications. In this chapter, we will explore how to secure your Go applications using the crypto package and best practices for writing secure Go code. We will cover the fundamentals of cryptography in Go, delve into hashing and encryption, learn how to generate secure random numbers, and understand how to handle user authentication and authorization with JWT.

Code Bundle and Coloured Images

Please follow the link to download the
Code Bundle and the *Coloured Images* of the book:

https://rebrand.ly/zt1vbph

The code bundle for the book is also hosted on GitHub at
https://github.com/bpbpublications/Get-Set-Go.
In case there's an update to the code, it will be updated on the existing GitHub repository.

We have code bundles from our rich catalogue of books and videos available at **https://github.com/bpbpublications**. Check them out!

Errata

We take immense pride in our work at BPB Publications and follow best practices to ensure the accuracy of our content to provide with an indulging reading experience to our subscribers. Our readers are our mirrors, and we use their inputs to reflect and improve upon human errors, if any, that may have occurred during the publishing processes involved. To let us maintain the quality and help us reach out to any readers who might be having difficulties due to any unforeseen errors, please write to us at :

errata@bpbonline.com

Your support, suggestions and feedbacks are highly appreciated by the BPB Publications' Family.

Did you know that BPB offers eBook versions of every book published, with PDF and ePub files available? You can upgrade to the eBook version at www.bpbonline.com and as a print book customer, you are entitled to a discount on the eBook copy. Get in touch with us at :

business@bpbonline.com for more details.

At **www.bpbonline.com**, you can also read a collection of free technical articles, sign up for a range of free newsletters, and receive exclusive discounts and offers on BPB books and eBooks.

Piracy

If you come across any illegal copies of our works in any form on the internet, we would be grateful if you would provide us with the location address or website name. Please contact us at **business@bpbonline.com** with a link to the material.

If you are interested in becoming an author

If there is a topic that you have expertise in, and you are interested in either writing or contributing to a book, please visit **www.bpbonline.com**. We have worked with thousands of developers and tech professionals, just like you, to help them share their insights with the global tech community. You can make a general application, apply for a specific hot topic that we are recruiting an author for, or submit your own idea.

Reviews

Please leave a review. Once you have read and used this book, why not leave a review on the site that you purchased it from? Potential readers can then see and use your unbiased opinion to make purchase decisions. We at BPB can understand what you think about our products, and our authors can see your feedback on their book. Thank you!

For more information about BPB, please visit **www.bpbonline.com**.

Join our book's Discord space

Join the book's Discord Workspace for Latest updates, Offers, Tech happenings around the world, New Release and Sessions with the Authors:

https://discord.bpbonline.com

Table of Contents

CHAPTER 1
Introduction to Go

Introduction

This chapter dives into the fundamentals of Go and explores the historical context behind its creation. It starts by uncovering the reasons that led to the development of the language and examines how its design addresses the challenges of large-scale software engineering. Key milestones in Go's evolution are highlighted, showcasing why it has become a go-to choice for modern software solutions. Along the way, we will examine the features that set Go apart, such as simplicity, efficiency, and effectiveness in building scalable and high-performance applications. Additionally, the chapter introduces the essential **fmt** package, demonstrating how it can be used to format and print output effectively.

Structure

This chapter covers the following topics:

- Introduction to Go and its history
- Setting up the Go environment
- Introduction to Go modules
- Writing and running your first Go program
- Format output using fmt package

Objectives

By the end of this chapter, you will understand the core principles behind Go's creation and the historical context that shaped its development. You will learn why Go was designed for simplicity, scalability, and performance, and how its features address the needs of modern software engineering. You will also explore Go's unique advantages in areas like concurrency, memory management, and cross-platform development. Additionally, you will be able to set up a Go development environment and gain insight into Go's key milestones and growing ecosystem.

Introduction to Go and its history

Go, often referred to as Golang, is a statically typed, compiled programming language. It is designed for simplicity, efficiency, and reliability. It was created by *Robert Griesemer*, *Rob Pike*, and *Ken Thompson* at *Google* and was first announced to the public in November 2009. The language was born out of a need to address the challenges of software development at scale, particularly within Google's vast infrastructure. Golang merges the performance of C with the simplicity and productivity of high-level languages like Python and Ruby.

Genesis of Go

The inception of Go can be traced back to late 2007 when the creators, frustrated with the complexity and inefficiency of existing languages, decided to design a new language. They wanted to create a language that could better meet the demands of modern software development. They aimed to create a language that combined the performance and safety of statically typed languages with the speed of dynamic languages.

Here are the key milestones of Go development:

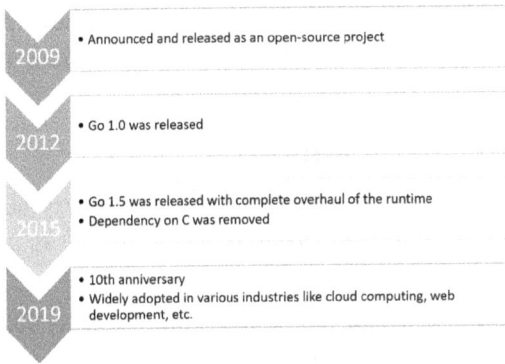

Figure 1.1: Key milestones of Go development

- **2009**: Go was officially announced and released as an open-source project. This release included a compiler, tools, and a standard library, setting the stage for community involvement and rapid evolution.

- **2012**: Go 1.0, the language's first stable version was released in 2012. It established a stable foundation for Go's syntax and semantics. It also ensured backward compatibility for future versions.

- **2015**: The release of Go 1.5 was significant as it included a complete overhaul of the runtime. It also removed the dependency on C and made Go a self-hosting language.

- **2019**: Go celebrated its 10th anniversary, with a thriving community. Go received widespread adoption in various industries, from cloud computing to web development and beyond. According to Go developer survey 2024 H2 results (**https://go.dev/blog/survey/2024-h2-results**), Go continues to enjoy strong developer satisfaction (93%), with ease of development and user-friendly APIs being key strength on major cloud platforms.

Why Go?

Go shines in scenarios where scalability, simplicity, and performance are key. It has become a popular choice for building modern web services, microservices, DevOps tools, and cloud-native applications. Go's strong support for concurrency makes it an excellent choice for applications requiring parallel processing. Its efficient memory usage helps in building high-performance servers and networked systems.

Go's impact and adoption

With a growing ecosystem and strong community support, Go has carved out a niche for itself as a language. It is particularly favoured in the following areas:

- **Cloud services**: Companies like Google, Docker, and Kubernetes use Go to build scalable and efficient cloud services.

- **Web development**: Go's performance and simplicity make it an excellent choice for web servers and APIs.

- **DevOps**: Tools like Terraform and Prometheus, which are essential in the DevOps ecosystem, are written in Go.

Key features of Go

Go has several features that make it an attractive choice for modern software development. We will take a look at them in this section.

Simplicity and clean syntax

Go is simple and has concise syntax. Go was designed to be easy to learn and read. The language avoids complex abstractions like inheritance, operator overloading, and implicit type conversion, promoting clarity in code.

Statically typed with type inference

Go is a statically typed language. This means variable types are checked at compile time. This provides more safety and preventing many types of bugs.

However, Go also supports type inference, allowing the compiler to automatically infer the type of variables based on the values assigned to them.

Let us look at this example:

```
var a int = 10
b := 20 // type inferred as int
```

Here, **a** is explicitly defined as an integer, while **b** is automatically inferred as an integer.

Efficient concurrency model

Go provides built-in support for concurrent programming through goroutines and channels. **Goroutines** are lightweight threads, managed by the Go runtime, and consume very little memory. This allows us to run thousands of concurrent tasks in parallel. Goroutines work in tandem with **channels**, which enable safe communication between them. This concurrency model simplifies the process of writing concurrent programs. It also avoids common issues like deadlocks and race conditions. This makes it easier to run multiple tasks simultaneously and leverage multi-core processors.

Goroutines and channels enable efficient concurrency, as evidenced by benchmarks (Golang vs. other languages, **https:// benchmarksgame-team.pages.debian.net/benchmarksgame/ fastest/go.html**).

Garbage collection

Go does automatic garbage collection. This means the Go runtime takes care of memory allocation and deallocation. Unlike C and C++, this relieves developers of the need to manually manage memory. Go's garbage collector is highly efficient and does not impact performance significantly. The garbage collection is optimized for latency and scalability. It is crucial for building web servers, microservices, and large-scale systems.

Fast compilation and execution

Unlike interpreted languages like Python and Ruby, Go is compiled. It converts code directly into machine code before execution. This results in faster execution and better performance. Go's compiler compiles large codebases quickly, even in projects with thousands of source files. The fast compilation and execution make Go ideal for scenarios where performance is critical.

Robust standard library

Go comes with an extensive standard library that simplifies common tasks, such as working with files, handling network operations, manipulating data, and creating web servers. The standard library is highly modular. We can import only the required packages keeping the code clean and efficient.

Though it is hard to count the number of modules and packages, the Go module index has about 1 million module paths.

Cross-platform and easy deployment

Go simplifies the process of building cross-platform applications. The Go compiler supports cross-compilation, which enables us to build binaries for different operating systems and processor architectures from a single codebase without modifying the code.

Additionally, Go compiles programs into single, statically linked binaries with no external dependencies. This makes deployment easy, as we do not need to deploy any additional libraries on the target machine.

Error handling with explicit errors

Go's approach to error handling is simple and explicit. Instead of exceptions, Go encourages developers to return errors as values. This makes error handling predictable and forces developers to handle errors in a clear and concise manner. This way of error handling improves the robustness of programs.

Strong community and ecosystem

Go has a large and active community that contributes by building libraries, tools, and frameworks. This means we can find high-quality third-party packages for a variety of use cases, from web development to machine learning. Popular frameworks like *Gin Gonic* (**https://github.com/gin-gonic/gin**) for web applications and **Go-kit** (**https://github.com/go-kit/kit**) for microservices are a few examples of the frameworks.

Setting up the Go environment

Before you can start writing Go code, you need to set up the development environment. Follow these steps to install Go on your system:

1. Download Golang from **https://golang.org/dl/** and install it following the instructions for your operating system.

2. Choose one of the popular IDEs/Text editors like **VS Code (https://code.visualstudio.com/)**, **GoLand (https://www.jetbrains.com/go/)**, **Atom (https://atom-editor.cc/)** or **Sublime Text (https://www.sublimetext.com/)**. It entirely depends on your personal preference.

3. Install additional tools like **GoDoc (https://go.dev/blog/godoc)** and **GoLint (https://pkg.go.dev/golang.org/x/lint/golint)** to view documentation and to lint your code.

Installing Golang

Let us now look into the steps to setup Golang:

1. Visit the official **Go Downloads** page: **https://golang.org/dl/**. Refer to the following figure (as of February 2, 2025):

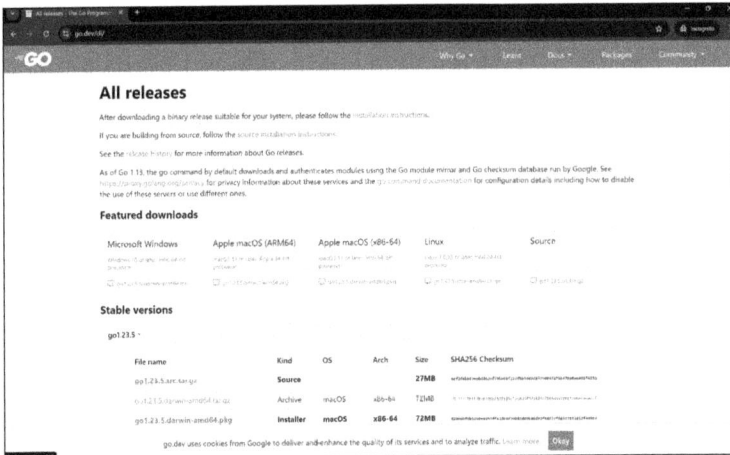

Figure 1.2: *Download Golang*

2. Based on your operating system (Windows, MacOS, or Linux) and system architecture (like amd64 for x64 systems), choose the appropriate distribution.

Follow the given steps to install Golang:

1. Windows:

   a. Open the downloaded **.msi** file.

    b. Follow the installation wizard, leaving default settings as they are unless you have a specific need.

2. macOS:

    a. Open the downloaded **.pkg** file.

    b. Follow the prompts in the installation wizard.

3. Linux:

    a. Open a terminal.

    b. Navigate to the directory where the **.tar.gz** file was downloaded.

    c. Extract the archive using **tar-xvf go$VERSION.$OS-$ARCH.tar.gz**.

    d. Move the extracted files to **/usr/local** using **sudo mv go /usr/local**.

    e. Open your **~/.bashrc** or **~/.zshrc** file in a text editor.

    f. Add the following line to the end of the file:

       `export PATH=$PATH:/usr/local/go/bin`

    g. Save and close the file.

    h. Refresh your profile with **source ~/.bashrc** or **source ~/.zshrc**.

4. Verify the installation:

    a. Open a terminal or command prompt.

    b. Type **go version** and press *Enter*.

    c. You should see the version number of Go displayed, indicating a successful installation.

5. Setting up a workspace:

    a. While Go modules (from Go 1.11 onwards) have made it less necessary to have a strict directory structure, traditionally Go developers set up a workspace. This can still be useful:

       i. Create a directory for your workspace, commonly named **go_workspace** in the home directory.

    ii. Inside this directory, create three subdirectories: **src**, **bin**, and **pkg**.

    iii. Set the **GOPATH** environment variable to point to your workspace directory. You can add this to your **~/.bashrc** or equivalent:

```
export GOPATH=$HOME/go_workspace
export PATH=$PATH:$GOPATH/bin
```

Choosing an IDE

While any text editor can be used, some IDEs enhance the Go coding experience:

- **Visual Studio Code (https://code.visualstudio.com/)**: Free, with a rich Go extension available.

- **GoLand (https://www.jetbrains.com/go/)**: JetBrains' specialized Go IDE, offers an extensive suite of tools and features.

Remember to install the Go plugin or extension suitable for your chosen IDE.

Introduction to Go modules

Go modules are the standard way to manage dependencies in Go projects. They allow us to specify the versions of the packages our project depends on. This ensures consistent builds.

They provide a robust and flexible mechanism for:

- **Version dependencies**: Explicitly specify and manage the versions of external packages.

- **Simplify dependency management**: Automate fetching, resolving, and updating dependencies.

- **Ensure reproducibility**: Guarantee consistent builds across different environments.

- **Isolate dependencies**: Create clear boundaries between your project and external libraries.

Key components include the **go.mod** file (declaring module path, version, and dependencies) and the **go.sum** file (recording dependency content).

By using modules, you enhance build consistency, improve project portability, and simplify project maintenance.

Creating a new module

To create a new Go module, navigate to your project directory and run:

```
go mod init <module-name>
```

This command creates a file, **go.mod** in the project directory, which will track the project's dependencies.

Writing and running your first Go program

Now that your environment is set up, let us write and run our first Go program. Follow the given steps:

1. **Create a new file**: Create a new file named **main.go** in your project directory and open it in your text editor.

2. **Write the code**: Add the following code to **main.go**:

   ```
   package main

   import "fmt"

   func main() {
       fmt.Println("Hello, Go!")
   }
   ```

3. **Run the program**: Save the file and run the following command in your terminal:

   ```
   go run main.go
   ```

You should see the following output:

```
Hello, Go!
```

Format output using fmt package

The **fmt** package is one of Go's most commonly used standard libraries.

A package in Go is a collection of related Go files that are compiled together, providing reusable code. Packages are necessary to promote modularity, code reuse, and maintainability.

The **fmt** package provides formatting functions for input and output, including printing to the console, reading from input, and creating formatted strings.

In this section, we will explore the basic usage of the package, focusing on how to use it for formatted output.

Basic printing functions

The **fmt** package has a few different functions for printing with subtle differences. They are:

- **fmt.Print()**: Prints the values passed to it without a newline.

- **fmt.Println()**: Prints the values followed by a newline.

- **fmt.Printf()**: Prints formatted output according to a format specifier.

Let us take a look at the following example:

```go
package main

import "fmt"

func main() {
    fmt.Print("Hello, ") // prints without newline
    fmt.Println("world!") // prints with a newline
    fmt.Printf("The number is %d.\n", 42) // formatted print
}
```

Here, the first **fmt** statement prints **"Hello"**, without a newline, so the next output appears on the same line. The next statement prints **"world!"** followed by a newline, moving the cursor to the next line. The final **fmt** statement prints the formatted string **"The number is 42"**. where **%d** is replaced by the integer **42**, and **\n** adds a newline at the end.

The output of this program is as shown:

```
Hello, world!
The number is 42.
```

Formatting with verbs

When using **fmt.Printf()**, format specifiers (verbs) allow us to control how the values are printed. Each verb corresponds to a specific type of data. Here are some common verbs:

- **%d**: Decimal integer
- **%f**: Floating-point number
- **%s**: String
- **%t**: Boolean
- **%v**: Default format for any value
- **%T**: Type of the value
- **%+v**: Value with field names (for structs)

Here is an example:

```go
package main

import "fmt"

type Person struct {
    Name string
    Age  int
}

func main() {
    fmt.Printf("Integer: %d\n", 100)
    fmt.Printf("Float: %.2f\n", 123.456) //
format float with 2 decimal places
    fmt.Printf("String: %s\n", "Go is fun")
    fmt.Printf("Boolean: %t\n", true)

    // Using %+v to display struct with field names
    p := Person{"Alice", 30}
    fmt.Printf("Struct: %+v\n", p)
    fmt.Printf("Type of variable p: %T\n", p)
}
```

The above program first prints an integer (**%d**), a floating-point number (**%.2f** to limit it to 2 decimal places), a string (**%s**), and a Boolean (**%t**). Then, it creates a **Person** struct and uses the **%+v** specifier to print the struct with its field names and **%T** to print the type of the **Person** variable **p**.

The output of this program is as follows:

```
Integer: 100
Float: 123.46
String: Go is fun
Boolean: true
Struct: {Name:Alice Age:30}
Type of variable p: main.Person
```

String formatting with Sprintf

If we need formatted output as a string rather than printing it directly, we can use **fmt.Sprintf()**. It works like **Printf()** but returns the formatted string.

Let us take a look at the following example:

```
package main

import «fmt"

func main() {
    name := "John"
    greeting := fmt.Sprintf("Hello, %s!", name)
    fmt.Println(greeting)
}
```

fmt.Sprintf creates a formatted string by inserting the value of the variable name into the placeholder **%s**, resulting in **"Hello, John!"**. The next line prints this formatted string to the console with a newline at the end.

Printing to other destinations

In addition to printing to the console, **fmt** can print to other destinations like files, buffers, or any type that implements the **io.Writer** interface. To print to a file, you would use **fmt.Fprintf()**.

Here is an example:

```
package main

import (
    "fmt"
    "os"
)
```

```go
func main() {
    file, err := os.Create("output.txt")
    if err != nil {
        panic(err)
    }
    defer file.Close()

    fmt.Fprintf(file, "This text is written to a file!\n")
}
```

In the above code, the main function creates a file named **output. txt** using **os.Create()**, which returns a file pointer file and an error, **err**. If an error occurs during file creation, **panic(err)** is called to halt the program and print the error. The defer **file. Close()** statement ensures that the file is properly closed once the function finishes executing. Finally, **fmt.Fprintf()** function writes the specified formatted string to the file.

Conclusion

In this chapter, we provided a comprehensive overview of Go, tracing its history and evolution from inception to its current status as a powerful programming language. We examined the key motivations behind its design, highlighting how Go addresses the challenges of modern software development. We learned how Go combines the performance of lower-level languages with the simplicity of higher-level ones. We also delved into Go's unique features that enhance productivity and efficiency, making it an excellent choice for a variety of applications. We guided you through the steps to set up your Go development environment, ensuring you are well-equipped to embark on your journey into the world of Golang. We also explored the fmt package, which helps us format and print the output.

In the next chapter we will dive into Go's data types and control structures. You will learn variables declaration, slices, and maps. We will also cover how to control the flow of programs using conditionals and loops.

CHAPTER 2

Data Types and Control Structures

Introduction

In this chapter, we will explore the core building blocks of Go, data types and control structures. We will cover Go's basic types—integers, floats, strings, and Booleans—and the concept of zero values. Zero values are default values assigned to uninitialized variables.

We will also dive into variable declaration methods using **var**, type inference, shorthand declarations, and variable scope. Composite types like arrays, slices, maps, and structs are explained, along with constants and enumerations using **iota**.

You will learn to manage program flow with conditional statements and looping constructs. Finally, we will address type conversions in Go's statically typed system. By the end, you will be well-versed in handling data and controlling program execution in Go.

Structure

This chapter covers the following topics:

- Basic data types
- Declaring and initializing variables
- Variable scope

- Composite data types
- Constants
- Enumerations
- Conditional statements
- Looping constructs

Objectives

In this chapter, you will be able to understand and work with Go's basic data types and recognize zero values as default initialization for variables. You will learn how to declare and initialize variables, type inference, and shorthand syntax (`:=`). You will also grasp the concept of variable scope. You will be equipped to work with composite data types and define constants and enumerations. Additionally, you will master conditional statements, use different types of loops, and perform explicit type conversions.

Basic data types

Go provides several basic data types, each serving a specific purpose:

- **Integers**: Represent whole numbers. They can be signed (`int`, `int8`, `int16`, `int32`, `int64`) or unsigned (`uint`, `uint8`, `uint16`, `uint32`, `uint64`).

- **Floats**: Represent numbers with fractional parts. Go supports **float32** and **float64**.

- **Strings**: A sequence of characters. Strings in Go are immutable.

- **Booleans**: Represent truth values, **true** or **false**.

Zero values

If a variable is declared without an explicit initial value, Go automatically assigns it a **zero value** based on its type. This behavior eliminates the need to explicitly initialize variables to default values like in some other languages.

The zero values for common types are:

- **int**: 0
- **float64**: 0.0
- **string**: "" (empty string)
- **bool**: false
- **pointers, slices, maps, channels, functions, interfaces**: nil

Declaring and initializing variables

Like any language, variables are a fundamental concept used to store and manipulate data. Understanding how to declare and initialize variables is crucial for writing effective Go programs. In this section, we will explore the different ways to declare and initialize variables, the types associated with them, and the scope of variables in Go.

The var keyword

The most explicit way to declare a variable in Go is by using the **var** keyword. You need to specify the variable's name, its type, and optionally initialize it with a value.

Here is the basic syntax of declaring a variable:

```
var variableName type = initialValue
```

If you do not initialize the variable, it will be given a zero value based on its type.

Let us look at this example:

```
package main

import "fmt"

func main() {
    // Declare a variable with an explicit type and value
    var age int = 30
    fmt.Println("Age:", age)
```

```
    // Declare a variable without an initial value (zero
value)
    var temperature float64
    fmt.Println("Temperature:", temperature)
}
```

In the example above, age is explicitly declared as an int and initialized with a value of **30**. The temperature variable is declared as a **float64** but is not initialized, so it holds Go's default **zero value** for a float, which is 0.0.

Type inference with var

Go allows for type inference. When we initialize a variable, Go can infer its type based on the assigned value. In this case, we can omit the type in the declaration.

```
package main

import "fmt"

func main() {
    var name = "Alice" // Go infers that 'name' is of type
string
    fmt.Println("Name:", name)
}
```

In the above code, the name is inferred to be of a type string based on the value **Alice**.

Shorthand declaration

Inside functions, Go provides a shorthand syntax for declaring and initializing variables using the := operator. This shorthand is only available **inside functions**.

The syntax of the shorthand declaration is like this:

```
variableName := initialValue
```

This is equivalent to using the **var** keyword with type inference but shorter and more concise.

Let us see this in action:

```
package main

import "fmt"
```

```
func main() {
    score := 100
    fmt.Println("Score:", score)
}
```

Here, the score is declared and initialized in one step. Go automatically infers that the type of score is int because 100 is an integer.

Note: The := syntax cannot be used outside of functions, for instance, at the package level.

Declaring multiple variables

Go allows for multiple variables to be declared at once, either using var or the shorthand :=. We can declare variables of the same or different types in a single line, as shown:

```
var a, b, c int = 1, 2, 3
var name, age, isEmployed = "John", 25, true
var (
    firstName string = "John"
    lastName  string = "Doe"
    age       int    = 30
    salary    float64
)
```

Here, **a**, **b**, and **c** are all declared as integers and initialized with values **1**, **2**, and **3**, respectively. In the next line, name is inferred as a string, **age** as an int, and **isEmployed** as a bool. Go automatically infers their types from the initialized values.

Alternatively, we can group variable declarations into a block, which makes the code more readable. In the last block in the code, multiple variables are declared in a single block. **firstName** and **lastName** are initialized, while salary is declared but holds the default zero value for **float64** (which is 0.0).

Variable scope

The scope of a variable in Go defines where the variable can be accessed in your program. Go has two main scopes, which we will discuss in this section.

Package-level scope

Variables declared outside of functions are visible throughout the entire package. These variables are sometimes referred to as global variables.

Package-level variables can be accessed by any function or method in the same package. They remain in memory for the lifetime of the program, and therefore, their values persist across different function calls. Refer to the following:

```
var packageLevelVar int = 50
func main() {
    fmt.Println(packageLevelVar) // Accessible
}
```

In this example, **packageLevelVar** is declared at the package level, making it accessible in **main()**. Any function within the **main** package can read or modify **packageLevelVar**.

Local scope

Local variables are declared inside functions and are only accessible within that function. Each function has its own set of local variables, which are created when the function is invoked and destroyed when the function completes execution. Refer to the following:

```
func func1() {
    var localVar int = 20
    fmt.Println(localVar) // Accessible
}

func func2() {
    fmt.Println(localVar) // Error: localVar is not
accessible here
}
```

In this example, **localVar** is declared inside the **func1()** function. It is only accessible within that function and cannot be accessed in **func2()**.

Composite data types

Composite data types allow us to group multiple values together into a single entity. These types are essential for working with collections of values that represent real-world objects. Go provides several composite data types, each serving different use cases: arrays, slices, maps, and structs.

Composite data types follow a similar variable declaration approach as basic data types, making them easy to work with once you're familiar with the basics.

We will take a look at them in this section.

Arrays

An array is a fixed-length collection of elements, all of the same type. Once an array is declared, its size cannot be changed. Hence, arrays offer predictable performance and memory usage.

We declare an array by specifying the number of elements and the type of elements it will hold:

```
var numbers [5]int = [5]int{1, 2, 3, 4, 5}
```

Here, **numbers** is an array of integers with a fixed size of 5. It is initialized with the values 1 through 5.

If we try to add or remove elements from this array, we will encounter a compile-time error because arrays in Go have a fixed size.

Slices

Slices are a more flexible and powerful alternative to arrays. Unlike arrays, slices are dynamically sized. They can grow or shrink as needed. Internally, slices are built on top of arrays but can change their size.

We declare a slice similarly to an array but without specifying its size:

```
var fruits []string = []string{"apple", "banana",
"cherry"}

fruits = append(fruits, "papaya")
fmt.Println(fruits) // Output: [apple banana cherry papaya]
```

Here, **fruits** is a slice of strings initialized with three elements. Then, we add an element to the slice **fruits** using the built-in **append()** function.

Maps

Maps are collections of key-value pairs, similar to dictionaries in other languages like Python. Maps allow us to store data where each element is associated with a unique key. It is easy to retrieve, insert, or delete elements based on the key of the pair.

We declare a **map** by specifying the types for the keys and values:

```go
var capitals map[string]string = map[string]string{
    "France": "Paris",
    "Japan":  "Tokyo",
}

capitals["Germany"] = "Berlin"
fmt.Println(capitals["France"])  // Output: Paris
fmt.Println(capitals["Germany"]) // Output: Berlin

city, exists := capitals["Italy"]
if exists {
    fmt.Println(city)
} else {
    fmt.Println("Key not found")
}
```

Here, **capitals** is a map where both the keys and values are **strings**. The key represents the name of a country, and the value represents its capital city. Then, we added another key-value pair, **Germany-Berlin**.

We also checked for the existence of the key **Italy**. To check if a key exists in a map, we use the second return value (**exisits**) from the map lookup, which is a Boolean indicating whether the key was found.

Structs

Structs allow us to define custom data types that group multiple fields together. Structs can hold data of different types to represent real-world objects. Refer to the following:

```go
type Car struct {
    Brand string
    Model string
    Year  int
```

```
}
myCar := Car{Brand: "Toyota", Model: "Corolla",
        Year: 2020}
fmt.Println(myCar.Brand) // Output: Toyota
```

Here, **Car** is a struct with three fields: **Brand** (a string), **Model** (a string), and **Year** (an integer). **myCar** is an instance of the **Car** struct, initialized with the values.

Constants

Constants represent fixed values that cannot be changed after they are defined. These values are known at compile time. This means constant values are determined before the program is run.

Constants can be declared using the **const** keyword. Unlike variables, constants cannot be declared using the shorthand **:=** syntax. Refer to the following:

```
const Pi = 3.14159
```

Enumerations

Go does not have a built-in enumeration (**enum**) type, but it provides a special keyword **iota** to create enumerated constants. **iota** simplifies the creation of incrementing values.

Let us look at the following code enumerating weekdays:

```
type Weekday int
const (
    Sunday Weekday = iota
    Monday
    Tuesday
    Wednesday
    Thursday
    Friday
    Saturday
)
```

Here, the **iota** keyword automatically increments each successive constant. **Sunday** is set to **0**, **Monday** to **1**, and so on. This approach is useful for creating enumerated values that are sequential.

Conditional statements

Control structures allow us to define the logic and flow of programs. Conditional statements are used to make decisions based on whether certain conditions are true or false.

If-else

The if statement in Go evaluates a Boolean expression. If the expression is true, the code inside the block is executed. An optional else block can handle the case where the condition is false.

To understand the construct of if-else, we will consider the following example:

```
// Get the current hour
currentTime := time.Now()
hour := currentTime.Hour()
// greeting based on the current hour
if hour >= 5 && hour < 12 {
 fmt.Println("Good Morning!")
} else if hour >= 12 && hour < 17 {
 fmt.Println("Good Afternoon!")
} else if hour >= 17 && hour < 21 {
 fmt.Println("Good Evening!")
} else {
 fmt.Println("Good Night!")
}
```

Here, **time.Now()** retrieves the current date and time. **Hour()** is a method that extracts just the hour (0-23) from the current time, which we store in the variable hour.

Then, in **if, else if,** and **else** block, we have the following checks:

- If the hour is between 5 AM and 12 PM, the program prints **"Good Morning!"**.

- If the hour is between 12 PM and 5 PM, it prints **"Good Afternoon!"**.

- If the hour is between 5 PM and 9 PM, it prints **"Good Evening!"**.

- For all other times, it prints **"Good Night!"**.

Switch

The switch statement provides a cleaner alternative to multiple if-else statements. It compares the value of a variable or expression against multiple possible cases and executes the code for the matching case.

We can use the switch in the following way:

```
switch day {
case "Monday":
    fmt.Println("Start of the work week")
case "Friday":
    fmt.Println("End of the work week")
case "Saturday", "Sunday":
    fmt.Println("Weekend")
default:
    fmt.Println("Midweek")
}
```

In this example, the switch statement compares the value of the day to each case:

- If day is **"Monday"**, it prints **"Start of the work week"**.
- If day is **"Friday"**, it prints **"End of the work week"**.
- If day is **"Saturday"** or **"Sunday"**, it prints **"Weekend"**.
- If no cases match, the default case is executed.

Looping constructs

Loops help us to execute a block of code multiple times, either a fixed number of times or based on a condition. Go provides the for loop as its only looping construct, but it can be used in different ways to achieve various forms of iteration.

Traditional for loop

The traditional for loop in Go works similarly to loops in languages like C or Java. It consists of three parts: an initialization, a condition, and an increment.

Here is a simple example:

```
for i := 0; i < 5; i++ {
```

```
    fmt.Println(i)
}
```

Here, the loop starts with **i** initialized to **0**. The condition **i < 5** ensures the loop runs while **i** is less than **5**. After each iteration, **i** is incremented by **1**. The loop will output the numbers **0** through **4**, each on a new line.

While-like for loop

Go does not have a while loop, but the for loop can mimic its behavior by omitting the initialization and increment sections. Golang does not have a dedicated **while** keyword because the **for** loop is incredibly versatile. It can effectively emulate any **while** loop behavior.

In the following code, the loop behaves like a **while** loop, continuing to execute as long as the condition (**i < 5**) is true:

```
i := 0
for i < 5 {
    fmt.Println(i)
    i++
}
```

Here, the loop continues to run as long as **i** is less than **5**. The statement **i++** increments the value of **i** after each iteration, ensuring that the loop progresses toward the termination condition.

It is crucial to increment **i** inside the loop; otherwise, the condition **i < 5** will always remain true, resulting in an infinite loop.

Range

The range keyword is used to iterate over elements in collections like arrays, slices, maps, and strings. It provides an easy way to loop through each element in the collection.

In the following code, range fruits iterates over the fruits slice. The loop returns two values: **index** and **value**:

```
fruits := []string{"apple", "banana", "cherry"}

for index, value := range fruits {
    fmt.Printf("%d: %s\n", index, value)
}
```

Using **range** over directly manipulating the index provides the following advantages:

- **Simplicity**: The range automatically handles the indexing and value retrieval, reducing boilerplate code.

- **Readability**: The code is cleaner and easier to understand, as it clearly shows the intent of iterating through a collection.

- **Reduced risk of errors**: It eliminates common mistakes such as off-by-one errors or accidentally modifying the loop counter.

- **Versatility**: range works seamlessly with different data types like slices, arrays, maps, and even strings, making it a consistent tool for iteration.

Type conversions

Go is a statically typed language, meaning that every variable has a specific type, and we cannot assign a value of one type to a variable of another type without explicitly converting it.

To convert between types, Go provides functions like **int()**, **float64()**, etc. You must perform conversions explicitly when needed. Refer to the following:

```
var x int = 42
var y float64 = float64(x)
```

Here, the integer **x** is converted to a **float64** before being assigned to **y**.

Understanding type conversion is crucial for writing robust Go programs. Let us explore why it is needed, how it applies to composite types, and the role of type safety in Go:

- **Need of type conversion**: Since Go enforces strict type safety, operations between incompatible types (e.g., **int** and **float64**) are not allowed without explicit conversion. This prevents unintended data loss, logic errors, or unpredictable behaviour.

- **Type conversion with composite types**: Conversion is only allowed when the composite types have the same underlying structure and element types. For example, two slices of different element types cannot be directly converted. However, for structs, even if they have identical fields, they must be explicitly defined as convertible in the code. Here is an example with arrays:

```
type A [3]int
type B [3]int

var a A = [3]int{1, 2, 3}
// var b B = a        // This will cause an error
var b B = B(a)        // Explicit conversion works
```

Here, **A** and **B** are defined as distinct array types, even though they have the same underlying structure (**[3] int**). We cannot assign **a** of type **A** directly to **b** of type **B** because Go enforces strict type safety. However, we can perform an explicit conversion using **B(a)** to convert a to type **B**, which allows the assignment.

- **Role of type safety**: Type safety refers to the enforcement of rules that prevent operations between incompatible data types. In Go, this ensures that variables hold and operate on data in ways that are predictable and safe. Type safety reduces the chances of runtime errors, data corruption, and unexpected behaviour.

Conclusion

In this chapter, we explored Go's foundational elements, data types, and control structures. We covered basic data types—integers, floats, strings, Booleans—and zero values. We learned how to declare and initialize variables and type inference. We also understood the importance of variable scope. We examined composite data types, as well as constants and iota for enumerations. Finally, we explored control structures like if-else, switch, and for loop for controlling program flow.

In the next chapter, we will discuss functions, their syntax, passing arguments, and returning values. We will also learn Go's approach to error handling.

CHAPTER 3

Functions and Error Handling

Introduction

In Go, functions are a fundamental component of building any application. They enable code reusability, modularity, and organization. Understanding how to declare and use functions is key to writing clean and maintainable code. This chapter covers the syntax for declaring functions, different types of parameters, and return values. It also touches upon advanced concepts like variadic functions, anonymous functions, closures, and error handling. By mastering these topics, you will be equipped to write more flexible and reliable code in Go.

We will also dive into error handling topics like throwing errors, defining, and handling custom errors.

Structure

This chapter covers the following topics:

- Function declaration and syntax
- Parameters and return values
- Variadic functions
- Anonymous functions and closures
- First-class and higher-order functions
- Defer, panic, and recover
- Error handling

Objectives

By the end of this chapter, you will be able to apply Go's function features to real-world scenarios. You will know how to write reusable, modular functions that simplify complex tasks, manage variable arguments using variadic functions, and create dynamic behaviours with anonymous functions and closures. You will also be capable of enhancing code reliability through effective error handling using defer, panic, and recover mechanisms. This knowledge will help you build robust applications, streamline debugging, and improve code maintainability in practical development environments.

Function declaration and syntax

Functions are the building blocks of any Go program. In Go, a function is declared using the **func** keyword followed by the function name, a list of parameters (with their types), and the return type(s). They have been explained as follows:

- **Function name**: Must start with a letter and can contain letters and numbers. Here are a few examples of function names:

```go
func add(a int, b int) int {
    return a + b
}
func multiplyBy2(n int) int {
    return n * 2
}
```

- **Parameter types**: You can define multiple parameters, and if consecutive parameters share the same type, you can omit repeating the type.

```go
func subtract(a, b int) int {
    return a - b
}
func divide(a, b float64) float64 {
    if b == 0 {
        return 0
    }
```

```
    return a / b
}
func greet(name string, age int) {
    fmt.Printf("Hello %s, you are %d years
old.\n", name, age)
}
```

In **subtract** and **divide** functions, both **a** and **b** are of type **int** and **float64** respectively. The function **greet** takes two parameters of different types, **name** (a string) and **age** (an integer).

- **Return types**: Go supports multiple **return** values, making it easier to return results along with error handling. Let us look at a few examples:

```
func add(a int, b int) (int, error) {
    if b == 0 {
        return 0, fmt.Errorf("Cannot add zero")
    }
    return a + b, nil
}
func splitName(fullName string) (string, string) {
    parts := strings.Split(fullName, " ")
    return parts[0], parts[1]
}
func getUserDetails(id int) (name string, age
int, error) {
    // Assume there's logic to retrieve details
    return "John Doe", 30, nil
}
```

Here, the **add** function returns two values: the **sum** and an **error**. If **b** is zero, an error is returned; otherwise, the **sum** is returned with **nil** indicating no error. The **splitName** function returns two strings. The **getUserDetails** function's return values are named (**name, age**). This approach improves clarity, especially in longer functions.

Parameters and return values

Go functions can be as simple as those with no parameters or return values, or as complex as those with multiple parameters and multiple return values. Understanding how parameters are passed and values returned is crucial for writing efficient Go programs. Following are a couple of key concepts to understand when working with functions in Go:

- **Pass-by-value**: By default, Go passes parameters by value. This means a copy of the variable is passed to the function. Any changes made within the function do not affect the original variable.

Let us look at this example:

```go
func modifyValue(x int) {
    x = 100 // Modifies the copy, not the original
}
func main() {
    num := 50
    fmt.Println("Before function call:", num)

    modifyValue(num)
    fmt.Println("After function call:", num)
}
```

In this code, the variable **num** is passed to the **modifyValue** function. Although **x** (a copy of **num**) is modified inside the function, the original **num** remains unchanged in **main()**. This demonstrates Go's pass-by-value behavior.

- **Multiple return values**: Go has the ability to return multiple values from a function. This is useful for functions that need to return both a result and an error.

Here is an example of multiple return values:

```go
func divide(a, b int) (int, error) {
    if b == 0 {
        return 0, errors.New("cannot divide
by zero")
    }
    return a / b, nil
}
func main() {
    result, err := divide(10, 2)
    if err != nil {
        fmt.Println("Error:", err)
```

```
    } else {
        fmt.Println("Result:", result)
    // Output: Result: 5
    }
    result, err = divide(10, 0)
    if err != nil {
        fmt.Println("Error:", err)
    // Output: Error: cannot divide by zero
    } else {
        fmt.Println("Result:", result)
    }
}
```

Here, the **divide** function returns two values: the result of the division and an error. If the divisor **b** is zero, it returns an error. Otherwise, it returns the division **result** and **nil** for the error. In **main()**, we check if an error occurred before using the result.

Variadic functions

A variadic function is one that can accept an indefinite number of arguments. Go provides a powerful feature for handling this using the ellipsis (**...**) syntax. This is especially useful for functions like **fmt.Println** that need to handle a variable number of inputs. Here are the essentials of variadic functions:

- **Declaration**: To define a variadic function, use **...** before the parameter type.

- **Same type arguments**: All arguments passed to a variadic function must be of the same type as defined in the function's parameter. To support mixed data types in variadic parameters an empty interface (**interface{}**) can be used. This allows any type but is less type-safe.

- **Practical use**: Variadic functions are ideal for scenarios where you want to pass a list of values of the same type but are not sure of the exact number.

In the following code, the **sum** function can accept any number of integers and return their sum. This eliminates the need for predefined limits on input size and simplifies code:

```
func sum(nums ...int) int {
    total := 0
    for _, num := range nums {
        total += num
    }
    return total
}
```

Anonymous functions and closures

Go supports anonymous functions, also known as **lambdas**. These are functions that do not have a name and are often used inline. When combined with closures, they become even more powerful. Let us take a look at them:

- **Anonymous functions**: These are commonly used for short operations or when passing functions as arguments.

```
func main() {
    increment := func(x int) int {
        return x + 1
    }
    fmt.Println(increment(5)) // Output: 6
}
```

This is an anonymous function because it has no name and is directly assigned to the variable **increment**.

- **Closures**: Closures are functions that reference variables from their surrounding scope. This makes them ideal for scenarios where you want to capture certain variables and use them later.

```
func main() {
    x := 5
    increment := func() int {
        x = x + 1
        return x
    }
    fmt.Println(increment()) // Output: 6
    fmt.Println(increment()) // Output: 7
}
```

In the preceding code, the variable **x** is declared outside the anonymous function **increment** and is part of the surrounding scope. The function captures x and modifies it each time increment is called. This makes it a closure because the function retains access to x, even after the scope where it was defined has passed.

First-class and higher-order functions

In Go, functions are first-class citizens, meaning they can be stored in variables, passed as arguments, and returned as results from other functions. Let us take a look at them:

- **First-class functions**: Functions can be assigned to variables, just like any other data type.

- **Higher-order functions**: These are functions that take other functions as parameters or return them. This allows for abstraction and the creation of more flexible code structures.

Refer to the following:

```go
package main

import "fmt"

// First-class function
var greet = func(name string) string {
    return "Hello, " + name
}

// Higher-order function
func processGreeting(f func(string) string, name string) {
    fmt.Println(f(name))
}

func main() {
    // Using the first-class function directly
    message := greet("Spock")
    fmt.Println(message) // Output: Hello, Spock

    // Passing the first-class function to a higher-order
function
    processGreeting(greet, "Ripley")
// Output: Hello, Ripley
}
```

In this program, the **greet** function is assigned to a variable, showcasing that functions **first-class citizens**. First class functions can be stored in variables, passed around, and used just like any other data type. This function takes a name as input and returns a greeting message. The **processGreeting** function is a **higher-order function** because it accepts another function (**f**) as an argument along with a string (**name**).

Inside **processGreeting,** the passed function is invoked with the provided name.

In the **main()** function, **greet** is first called directly with **"Spock"**, and then it is passed as an argument to **processGreeting** along with **"Ripley"**.

Defer, panic, and recover

Go provides a robust system for handling errors and unexpected conditions through the defer, panic, and recover mechanism.

Defer

It allows us to delay the execution of a function until the surrounding function returns. It is commonly used for resource cleanup, like closing files or network connections.

In the following code, **fmt.Println("This will be printed first")** executes immediately, printing its message first. The **defer** statement postpones the execution of **fmt.Println("This will be printed last")** until the main function returns, resulting in its message being printed last:

```go
func main() {
  defer fmt.Println("This will be printed last")
  fmt.Println("This will be printed first")
}
```

Panic and recover

Panics are triggered by unexpected situations, which immediately halt the normal execution flow. Recover is used to regain control of a program that is panicking. It helps us prevent the program from crashing. Recover only works when called inside a deferred function, allowing the program to handle the panic gracefully and continue execution where appropriate.

In the following code, the deferred function is set to run after the main function completes, even if a panic occurs. It handles the recovery. The call to **panic("Something went wrong!")** halts the normal execution flow and starts unwinding the stack, causing any deferred functions to run. Inside the deferred function, **recover()** is used to catch the panic and prevent the program from crashing:

```go
func main() {
    // defer ensures this function runs even after a panic
    defer func() {
        if r := recover(); r != nil {
            fmt.Println("Recovered from:", r)
        }
    }()

    fmt.Println("Starting the program")
    panic("Something went wrong!") // triggers a panic
    fmt.Println("This will not be printed")
// unreachable due to panic
}
```

Error handling

Error handling is an essential part of any robust application. Go provides a unique approach to error handling that is simple, clear, and encourages explicit error checking. Instead of exceptions or try-catch blocks found in other languages, Go uses multiple return values and the built-in error type for handling errors.

Basic error handling

In Go, it is common to return an error as the second return value from a function. The caller checks if the error is nil to determine if the operation was successful.

Here is a simple example:

```go
package main

import (
```

```
    "errors"
    "fmt"
)
func divide(a, b float64) (float64, error) {
    if b == 0 {
        return 0, errors.New("division by zero")
    }
    return a / b, nil
}
func main() {
    result, err := divide(4, 0)
    if err != nil {
        fmt.Println("Error:", err)
        return
    }
    fmt.Println("Result:", result)
}
```

In the above code, the **divide** function returns two values: the result of the division and an error. If **b** is zero, the function returns an error using the **errors.New** function. In main, the error is checked. If there is an error, it is handled, and the program terminates early.

Creating custom errors

Go allows us to create custom error types by implementing the error interface. The interface simply requires a method with the following signature:

```
type error interface {
    Error() string
}
```

This helps us create a custom error type. Let us see how that works:

```
package main

import (
    "fmt"
)

// Custom error type
type DivideError struct {
    Dividend float64
```

```
    Divisor   float64
}
func (e *DivideError) Error() string {
    return fmt.Sprintf("cannot divide %.2f by %.2f", e.
Dividend, e.Divisor)
}
func divide(a, b float64) (float64, error) {
    if b == 0 {
        return 0, &DivideError{Dividend: a, Divisor: b}
    }
    return a / b, nil
}
func main() {
    _, err := divide(4, 0)
    if err != nil {
        fmt.Println("Error:", err)
    }
}
```

This code defines a custom error type **DivideError,** to handle division by zero. In the **divide** function, if the divisor **b** is zero, it returns an instance of **DivideError** with the dividend and divisor values, using the **Error()** method to format the error message. If the division is valid, it returns the result. In the **main** function, when **divide(4, 0)** is called, an error is triggered and printed as **Error: cannot divide 4.00 by 0.00**.

Checking error types

Another useful tool is **errors.As**, which checks if an error is of a specific type. This is particularly useful for custom errors.

The following is almost the same code that we had used to explain custom error types except for the fact that we handle the error this time. The function **errors.As** checks if the error is of a certain type (in this case, **DivideError**) and extracts it. This way, we allow you to handle specific error types:

```
package main

import (
    "errors"
    "fmt"
)
```

```go
type DivideError struct {
    Dividend float64
    Divisor  float64
}
func (e *DivideError) Error() string {
    return fmt.Sprintf("cannot divide %.2f by %.2f",
e.Dividend, e.Divisor)
}
func divide(a, b float64) (float64, error) {
    if b == 0 {
        return 0, &DivideError{Dividend: a, Divisor: b}
    }
    return a / b, nil
}
func main() {
    _, err := divide(4, 0)
    if err != nil {
        var divideErr *DivideError
        if errors.As(err, &divideErr) {
            fmt.
Println("Caught a DivideError:", divideErr)
        }
    }
}
```

Conclusion

In this chapter, we delved into the essential components of Go functions, including their declaration and syntax. We explored the use of parameters, return types, and how Go efficiently handles multiple return values. Additionally, we learned about more advanced concepts such as variadic functions, anonymous functions, and closures, which provide greater flexibility in coding. Finally, we covered Go's approach to error handling and the use of higher-order functions. With this foundational understanding, you are now equipped to write efficient, maintainable, and robust Go functions.

The next chapter covers string manipulation and file handling. It explores the strings and os packages. It also delves into file and directory management and command-line arguments.

CHAPTER 4

Strings and Files

Introduction

In this chapter, we will delve into two fundamental aspects of programming in Go: string manipulation and file handling. This chapter explores Go's built-in packages, the strings and os packages. We will discuss essential string manipulation functions, UTF-8 encoding, and immutable string behavior. Additionally, we will dive into file and directory handling, which is essential for managing data storage, creating files and directories, and handling input and output operations. Command-line arguments will also be covered. It gives us the flexibility to interact with programs directly from the terminal. Together, these topics provide a strong foundation for building powerful applications in Go.

Structure

This chapter covers the following topics:

- String manipulation
- Basic file operations
- Command-line arguments

Objectives

By the end of this chapter, you will be able to understand the basics of strings in Go, including their immutability and UTF-8 encoding, and how these properties impact string manipulation. You will learn to utilize functions from the **strings** package for common operations. Additionally, you will gain the skills to implement file handling techniques to read from and write to files. You will also explore how to manage directories and paths using the **os** and **path/filepath** packages. This will help you to create, delete, and navigate directories in a cross-platform manner. Furthermore, you will learn to capture and process command-line arguments. Ultimately, you will be able to integrate string manipulation, file handling, and command-line argument processing into cohesive Go programs.

String manipulation

Go provides a rich set of tools for working with strings. Let us explore the strings package, which offers a variety of functions for string manipulation.

Understanding strings

Strings in Go are known for their immutability and UTF-8 encoding. This makes strings both memory-efficient and compatible with a wide range of international text. Let us explore the core aspects of Go strings with examples.

Immutable nature

In Go, strings are immutable, meaning they cannot be changed once created. Any operation that seems to modify a string will instead create a new string, leaving the original unchanged. This makes it thread-safe and memory-efficient but has implications when performing many modifications in succession.

In the following code, the main goal is to modify the string **str** by changing its first character from uppercase **"H"** to lowercase **"h"**. Since strings in Go are immutable, attempting to directly change **str[0]** would cause a compilation error, as noted in the comment. Instead, a new string **newStr** is created by concatenating **"h"** with the substring **str[1:]**.

```
package main

import "fmt"

func main() {
  str := "Hello"
  // Attempting to modify string directly causes an error
  // str[0] = 'h' // This throws a compile-time error

  // Instead, we create a new string
  newStr := "h" + str[1:]
  fmt.Println(newStr) // Output: "hello"
}
```

UTF-8 encoding

Go strings are UTF-8 encoded. This makes it easier to handle characters from multiple languages.

The following program iterates over a Unicode string containing Hindi and English characters, नमस्ते, **Go!**, and prints each character with its position and Unicode code point. The **for** loop uses **range**, handling a **rune** (Unicode code point) at a time. For each character **r** in the string **str**, we print the character's position **i**, the character itself as **%c**, and its Unicode value as **%U**. This approach ensures proper handling of multilingual text in Go:

```
package main

import "fmt"

func main() {
  str := "नमस्ते, Go!"
  for i, r := range str {
    fmt.Printf("Character %d: %c (Unicode: %U)\n", i, r, r)
  }
}
```

The program outputs the following:

```
Character 0: न (Unicode: U+0928)
Character 3: म (Unicode: U+092E)
Character 6: स (Unicode: U+0938)
Character 9: ् (Unicode: U+094D)
Character 12: त (Unicode: U+0924)
```

```
Character 15: ☒ (Unicode: U+0947)
Character 18: , (Unicode: U+002C)
Character 19:   (Unicode: U+0020)
Character 20: G (Unicode: U+0047)
Character 21: o (Unicode: U+006F)
Character 22: ! (Unicode: U+0021)
```

Basic string operations

Go's **strings** package is rich with functions for common string operations, including comparison, searching, splitting, joining, and replacing. Each function is designed for Go's UTF-8 encoded strings.

Here is an expanded look at these functions with examples:

```go
package main

import (
 "fmt"
 "strings"
)

func main() {
 // Checking if a string contains a substring
 fmt.Println("Contains example:")
 fmt.Println(strings.
Contains("Hello, Go!", "Go")) // Output: true

 // Counting occurrences of a substring
 fmt.Println("\nCount example:»")
 fmt.Println(strings.
Count("Hello, Go!", "o")) // Output: 2

 // Replacing substrings
 fmt.Println("\nReplaceAll example:»")
 fmt.Println(strings.ReplaceAll("Hello, Go!", "Go",
"Golang")) // Output: Hello, Golang!

 // Splitting a string
 fmt.Println("\nSplit example:»")
 words := strings.Split("Hello, Go!", ", ")
```

```
fmt.Println(words) // Output: [Hello Go!]

// Joining a slice of strings
fmt.Println("\nJoin example:»")
fmt.Println(strings.
Join(words, ", ")) // Output: Hello, Go!
}
```

The preceding program demonstrates common string manipulation functions from the **strings** package.

The **Contains** function verifies if **"Go"** is within **"Hello, Go!"**, outputting true. The **Count** function then counts how often **"o"** appears in the string, returning **2**. Using **ReplaceAll**, the program replaces **"Go"** with **"Golang"**, resulting in **"Hello, Golang!"**. The **Split** function breaks the string **"Hello, Go!"** into a slice of substrings at **", "**, producing **["Hello", "Go!"]**. Finally, **Join** reassembles these substrings with **", "** as the separator, recreating the original **"Hello, Go!"**.

Additional operations

The strings package also provides several other useful functions for handling text processing and manipulation tasks in a clean and readable way.

Checking prefix and suffix

The **HasPrefix** and **HasSuffix** functions are helpful for validating string patterns, such as file extensions or specific string formats. Here is an example demonstrating the usage of these functions:

```
package main
import (
 "fmt"
 "strings"
)
func main() {
 fmt.Println(strings.HasPrefix("golang.
org", "go")) // Output: true
 fmt.Println(strings.HasSuffix("golang.org", ".
org")) // Output: true
}
```

Converting case

Use **ToUpper** and **ToLower** to convert strings to uppercase or lowercase, which can standardize text for comparisons or formatting. Here is an example:

```
text := "Hello, Go!"
fmt.Println(strings.ToUpper(text)) // Output: "HELLO, GO!"
fmt.Println(strings.ToLower(text)) // Output: "hello, go!"
```

Here, **strings.ToUpper(text)** converts all the characters in the string **text** to uppercase, resulting in **"HELLO, GO!"**. Similarly, **strings.ToLower(text)** converts all characters in the string to lowercase, producing **"hello, go!"**.

Trimming whitespace and other characters

To clean strings by removing leading and trailing whitespace or specific characters, **TrimSpace** and **Trim** are invaluable. The following is a simple example:

```
text := "   Hello, Go!   "
fmt.Println(strings.
TrimSpace(text)) // Output: "Hello, Go!"
fmt.Println(strings.
Trim(text, " ")) // Output: "Hello, Go!"
```

Basic file operations

File handling allows programs to interact with data stored on disk. Go provides robust support for various file operations through the **os** and **io** packages. These packages help us open, read, write, and manage files and directories. This section will cover the key aspects of file handling in Go.

Opening and closing files

To work with files in Go, we first need to open them. The **os** package provides functions like **os.Open** and **os.Create** for this purpose. Note that **os.Create** truncates the file if it already exists, meaning it will clear its contents before writing new data. It is crucial to close files properly to free up system resources.

Go's defer statement can help with this by ensuring that the file is closed when the function returns.

In the following program, it attempts to open **"example.txt"** and prints an error message if unsuccessful. We use **defer** to ensure the file is closed afterward. It then tries to create a new file named **"newfile.txt"** and handles any errors similarly. If both operations succeed, it prints a success message.

```go
package main

import (
 "fmt"
 "os"
)
func main() {
 // Opening a file
 file, err := os.Open("example.txt")
 if err != nil {
  fmt.Println("Error opening file:", err)
  return
 }
 // Ensure the file is closed after we are done with it
 defer file.Close()

 // Creating a file
 newFile, err := os.Create("newfile.txt")
 if err != nil {
  fmt.Println("Error creating file:", err)
  return
 }
 defer newFile.Close()

 fmt.Println("Files opened and created!")
}
```

Reading and writing files

To read files, we can use **os.ReadFile** and **os.WriteFile** to read and write files, respectively. Let us look at an example:

```go
package main

import (
```

```
    "log"
    "os"
)
func main() {
    data, err := os.ReadFile("example.txt")
    if err != nil {
        log.Fatal(err)
    }

    log.Println(string(data))

    msg := []byte("\nWriting data to the file»)

    data = append(data, msg...)

    err = os.WriteFile("new_file.txt", data, 0744)
    if err != nil {
        log.Fatal(err)
    }
}
```

The preceding code demonstrates basic file reading and writing operations. It begins by reading the content of a file named **"example.txt"** using **os.ReadFile**. This loads the entire file content into memory as a byte slice (**data**). If an error occurs while reading, the error is logged, and the program is stopped. The file content is then printed to the console as a string.

Next, a new message (**msg**) is created as a byte slice. This message is appended to the original data. Finally, the modified data is written to a new file, **"new_file.txt"**, with permissions set to **0744**. The **0744** file mode grants read, write, and execute permissions to the owner (**7**), and read-only permissions to the group and others (**4 each**). If any error occurs during this write operation, it is also logged and handled.

Handling directories and file paths

In Go, directory and file path management is handled primarily by the **os** and **path/filepath** packages. These packages provide utilities for creating, deleting, and managing directories, as well as manipulating and navigating file paths in a cross-platform manner.

The following example covers creating a directory structure, writing files, retrieving paths, and recursively listing all files and directories within a specified root directory:

```go
package main
import (
    "fmt"
    "log"
    "os"
    "path/filepath"
)
func main() {
    rootDir := "exampleDir"
    nestedDir := filepath.Join(rootDir, "nestedDir")

    // Step 1: Create a root directory and a
nested directory
    if err := os.MkdirAll(nestedDir, 0755); err != nil {
        log.Fatalf("Error creating directories: %v", err)
    }
    fmt.Println("Directories created:", rootDir,
"and", nestedDir)

    // Step 2: Create a new file within the nested directory
    filePath := filepath.Join(nestedDir, "file.txt")
    fileContent := []byte("This is a sample file.")
    if err := os.WriteFile(filePath, fileContent, 0644);
err != nil {
        log.Fatalf("Error creating file: %v", err)
    }
    fmt.Println("File created:", filePath)

    // Step 3: Get absolute path for the nested directory
 and the file
    absRootDir, err := filepath.Abs(rootDir)
    if err != nil {
        log.Fatalf("Error getting absolute path: %v", err)
    }
    fmt.Println("Absolute path of root directory:",
absRootDir)

    absFilePath, err := filepath.Abs(filePath)
    if err != nil {
        log.Fatalf("Error getting absolute file path: %v",
 err)
```

```go
    }
    fmt.Println("Absolute path of file:", absFilePath)

    // Step 4: List all files and directories within
the root directory
    fmt.Println("Directory structure:")
    err = filepath.Walk(rootDir, func(path string,
info os.FileInfo, err error) error {
        if err != nil {
            return err
        }
        fmt.Println(" -", path)
        return nil
    })
    if err != nil {
        log.Fatalf("Error walking the directory tree: %v",
 err)
    }

    // Step 5: Clean up - Remove all directories
and files created
    if err := os.RemoveAll(rootDir); err != nil {
        log.Fatalf("Error removing directories: %v", err)
    }
    fmt.Println("Directories and files cleaned up.")
}
```

In this code, we have done the following operations:

- **Directory creation**: We create a **rootDir** directory and a nested **nestedDir** using **os.MkdirAll**, which creates all necessary directories in one step.

- **File creation**: Inside the nested directory, we create a file called **file.txt** and write sample content to it.

- **Path manipulation**: We use **filepath.Abs** to retrieve and print the absolute paths of the root directory and file, making the paths platform-independent.

- **Directory traversal**: Using **filepath.Walk**, we recursively list each file and directory within **rootDir**.

- **Cleanup**: Finally, **os.RemoveAll** removes the entire directory structure we created.

Command-line arguments

In Go, command-line arguments enable us to provide input to our programs from the terminal. This provides flexibility without modifying the code. The **os** package offers tools for capturing and working with these arguments.

Command-line arguments are available via **os.Args**, which returns a slice of strings. The first element, **os.Args[0]**, is the program name. Subsequent elements (**os.Args[1:]**) contain the arguments passed to the program.

Here is a simple example that shows how to capture and print command-line arguments in Go:

```go
package main

import (
    "fmt"
    "os"
)

func main() {
    args := os.Args // Capture all command-line arguments
    fmt.Println("Program Name:", args[0])
// Print the program name

    if len(args) > 1 {
        fmt.Println("Arguments passed:")
        for i, arg := range args[1:] {
            fmt.Printf("Argument %d: %s\n", i+1, arg)
        }
    } else {
        fmt.Println("No arguments provided.")
    }
}
```

The **os.Args** slice contains all arguments passed to the program, with the program name as the first element. The code starts by printing the program name. It then checks if any additional arguments were passed. If arguments are found, it iterates over them, printing each argument's index and value. Otherwise, it prints a message indicating that no arguments were received.

Running the program with **go run main.go hello world** will produce the following output:

```
Program Name: path/to/main
Arguments passed:
Argument 1: hello
Argument 2: world
```

Conclusion

In this chapter, we explored key techniques for working with strings, files, and directories in Go, along with handling command-line arguments. We started with the basics of string manipulation, focusing on the immutability of Go strings, UTF-8 encoding, and essential functions in the strings package. Next, we covered file handling, from opening and creating files to reading, writing, and managing directories with cross-platform path manipulation tools. We concluded by examining how to capture and use command-line arguments. Altogether, these topics have laid a strong foundation for handling text, data storage, and user input.

The following chapter delves into reflection. It allows developers to inspect and manipulate types and values at runtime.

Join our book's Discord space

Join the book's Discord Workspace for Latest updates, Offers, Tech happenings around the world, New Release and Sessions with the Authors:

https://discord.bpbonline.com

CHAPTER 5

Go Reflection

Introduction

Reflection in Go is a powerful feature that allows developers to inspect and manipulate types and values at runtime. This capability can make your code more dynamic and flexible. It enables you to write programs that can adapt to different types and structures without knowing them at compile time. In this chapter, we will explore the fundamentals of Go's reflect package, which provides the tools necessary for reflection. We will cover how to extract type information, work with values, and even modify them programmatically.

Structure

This chapter covers the following topics:

- Introduction to reflection
- Type and value introspection
- Kinds in reflection
- Modifying values with reflection

Objectives

This chapter will help you understand the fundamentals of reflection in Go. It includes reflection's role in examining and modifying a program's structure and behavior at runtime. You will learn about the **reflect** package and its key components—**reflect.Type** and **reflect.Value**. These are essential for type and value introspection. Additionally, you will gain the skills to modify basic types, struct fields, and slice elements dynamically using reflection. You will explore how to check for a type's kind and ensure that variables are settable before modifying them.

Introduction to reflection

Reflection allows a program to examine and modify its own structure and behavior at runtime. This is useful in scenarios where the code needs to handle unknown or dynamically defined types, such as in testing frameworks, or serialization processes.

In Go, reflection is facilitated by the **reflect** package. It provides the tools necessary to inspect types and values dynamically.

The reflect package

The reflect package in Go provides a set of functions and types that allow us to perform reflection. Key components of this package include **reflect.Type** and **reflect.Value**, which represent the type and value of a variable, respectively. Understanding these components is crucial for effectively using reflection in your Go programs.

Type and value introspection

Type introspection is the process of examining the type of a variable at runtime. With reflection, we can determine the type of any variable, regardless of whether it is a basic type, a struct, or an interface. This is particularly useful when writing functions that need to handle multiple types.

We will use the following code to understand the concept:

```
package main

import (
 «fmt"
```

```
«reflect»
)
func printTypeAndValue(i interface{}) {
 t := reflect.TypeOf(i)
 v := reflect.ValueOf(i)
 fmt.Printf("Type: %s, Value: %v\n", t, v)
}
func main() {
 printTypeAndValue(42)
 printTypeAndValue("Hello, Go!")
 printTypeAndValue(3.14)
}
```

In this example, the **printTypeAndValue** function takes an empty interface which allows it to accept any type. It then uses **reflect. TypeOf** and **reflect.ValueOf** to print the type and value of the argument.

The output of the program is as follows:

```
Type: int, Value: 42
Type: string, Value: Hello, Go!
Type: float64, Value: 3.14
```

Kinds in reflection

Every Go type falls under a specific **kind** (or category). The kind reflects its underlying representation in the language. Common kinds include **Struct, Int, Float, Slice, Map, Func,** and **Interface**.

Knowing a type's kind enables us to handle it appropriately in generic functions. For example, we may want to check if a value is a slice before iterating over its elements.

Here is how you can use the **Kind** method to determine and handle the kind of value:

```
package main

import (
 «fmt"
 «reflect»
```

```
)
func PrintValue(v interface{}) {
 val := reflect.ValueOf(v)
 switch val.Kind() {
 case reflect.Int:
  fmt.Printf("Integer: %d\n", val.Int())
 case reflect.String:
  fmt.Printf("String: %s\n", val.String())
 case reflect.Slice:
  fmt.Printf("Slice: %v\n", val.Interface())
 default:
  fmt.Println("Unsupported type")
 }
}
func main() {
 PrintValue(42)
 PrintValue("Hello, Go!")
 PrintValue([]int{1, 2, 3})
}
```

In the **PrintValue** function, **reflect.ValueOf** retrieves the reflection value of **v**. This value can then be checked for its kind (for example, **reflect.Int**, **reflect.String**, or **reflect.Slice**). A switch statement is used to handle different kinds, performing kind-specific operations: for an integer, it prints the integer value, for a string, it prints the string, and for a slice, it prints the slice elements using **Interface()**.

The output of the program is as follows:

```
Integer: 42
String: Hello, Go!
Slice: [1 2 3]
```

Modifying values with reflection

To modify a value through reflection, the variable needs to be settable. By setting values at runtime, we can build dynamic code that adapts based on the context.

This usually means passing a pointer to the variable.

Example: Modifying basic types

Let us start with a simple example that modifies an int and a string using reflection:

```go
package main

import (
 "fmt"
 "reflect"
)

func main() {
 var x int = 10
 var y string = "Hello"

 modifyValue(&x, 20)
 modifyValue(&y, "World")

 fmt.Println("Modified int:", x)     // Modified int: 20
 fmt.Println("Modified string:", y) // Modified string: World
}

func modifyValue(variable interface{},
newValue interface{}) {
 val := reflect.ValueOf(variable)

 // Check if the reflect.Value is a pointer and is settable
 if val.Kind() == reflect.Ptr && val.Elem().CanSet() {
  newVal := reflect.ValueOf(newValue)

  // Make sure the types match before setting the value
  if newVal.Type().AssignableTo(val.Elem().Type()) {
   val.Elem().Set(newVal)
  } else {
   fmt.Println("Type mismatch")
  }
 } else {
  fmt.Println("Value is not settable")
 }
}
```

The output is as follows:

```
Modified int: 20
Modified string: World
```

In **modifyValue**, the **reflect.ValueOf** function wraps the input variable in a reflection **Value**, allowing runtime inspection and manipulation. First, it checks if the variable is a pointer and if the underlying value (**Elem**) is settable/modifiable. If so, it creates a **reflect.Value** for **newValue**, confirming it is assignable to variable's type. If types are compatible, it assigns **newValue** to variable's underlying element. Otherwise, it displays error messages if the value is not settable or the types do not match, ensuring safe runtime modifications.

Example: Modifying struct fields

Now, let us work with a **struct** to modify its fields using reflection. This will allow us to create dynamic functions that can alter struct fields without knowing the exact **struct** type. Refer to the following:

```go
package main

import (
 "fmt"
 "reflect"
)

type Person struct {
 Name string
 Age  int
}

func main() {
 p := &Person{Name: "Alice", Age: 30}
 modifyField(p, "Name", "Bob")
 modifyField(p, "Age", 40)

 fmt.Printf("Modified Person: %+v\n", p) // Modified Person:
&{Name:Bob Age:40}
}
```

```go
func modifyField(s interface{}, fieldName string,
newValue interface{}) {
 val := reflect.ValueOf(s)

 // Ensure the reflect.Value is a pointer to a struct
 if val.Kind() == reflect.Ptr && val.Elem().Kind() ==
reflect.Struct {
  field := val.Elem().FieldByName(fieldName)

  // Check if the field is valid and settable
  if field.IsValid() && field.CanSet() {
   newVal := reflect.ValueOf(newValue)

   // Make sure the types are compatible
   if newVal.Type().AssignableTo(field.Type()) {
    field.Set(newVal)
   } else {
    fmt.Printf("Type mismatch: cannot assign %v to
field %s\n", newVal.Type(), fieldName)
   }
  } else {
   fmt.Printf("Field %s is not settable or does
not exist\n", fieldName)
  }
 } else {
  fmt.Println("Expected a pointer to a struct")
 }
}
```

The output is as follows:

Modified Person: &{Name:Bob Age:40}

The **modifyField** function takes a pointer to a struct, a field name, and a new value. Using **reflect.ValueOf**, it first checks if the input s is a pointer to a struct, allowing access to the struct's fields. Then, it retrieves the field by name using **FieldByName** and verifies if it exists (**IsValid()**) and is settable (**CanSet()**). If these checks pass, **modifyField** creates a reflection **Value** of **newValue**. When compatible, it sets the new value; otherwise, it outputs type mismatch or field accessibility errors, ensuring safe, controlled modification of struct fields.

Example: Modifying slice elements

Reflection is also useful for modifying individual elements in a slice. Here is how to use reflection to change values in a **slice** dynamically:

```go
package main

import (
 "fmt"
 "reflect"
)

func main() {
 numbers := []int{1, 2, 3, 4}
 modifySlice(&numbers, 2, 99)
 fmt.Println("Modified slice:", numbers)
}

func modifySlice(slice interface{}, index int,
newValue interface{}) {
 val := reflect.ValueOf(slice)

 // Ensure it's a pointer to a slice
 if val.Kind() == reflect.Ptr && val.Elem().Kind()
== reflect.Slice {
  sliceVal := val.Elem()
  elem := sliceVal.Index(index)

  // Make sure the element is settable and types match
  if elem.CanSet() && reflect.TypeOf(newValue).
AssignableTo(elem.Type()) {
   elem.Set(reflect.ValueOf(newValue))
  } else {
   fmt.Println("Cannot set element at index", index)
  }
 } else {
  fmt.Println("Expected a pointer to a slice")
 }
}
```

The output is as follows:

`Modified slice: [1 2 99 4]`

In **modifySlice**, the parameter **slice** is expected to be a pointer to a slice to allow direct modification of the original data. First, **reflect.ValueOf(slice)** retrieves the reflection **Value** of slice, and it checks if slice is a pointer to a slice. If true, it retrieves the slice's **reflect.Value** with **val.Elem()** and accesses the element at the specified index using **sliceVal.Index(index)**.

The code then verifies two conditions for setting the new value: that the element is settable (**elem.CanSet()**) and that the type of **newValue** matches the element's type (**AssignableTo**). If these conditions are met, **elem.Set** assigns **newValue** to the **slice** element. Otherwise, it outputs an error message if the element cannot be set or if the types do not match.

Conclusion

We delved into the essential techniques for utilizing reflection in Go. We covered its capabilities for introspecting and modifying program structure at runtime. We began by understanding the reflect package. We learned how to examine types and values dynamically. We then explored how to modify basic types, struct fields, and slice elements. Finally, we examined how to determine a type's kind to handle different data types effectively. By integrating these concepts, you now have a solid foundation for leveraging reflection in your Go programs.

In the next chapter, we will dive into Go's concurrency model and will explore goroutines, channels, and synchronization mechanisms. We will also discuss the context package.

Join our book's Discord space

Join the book's Discord Workspace for Latest updates, Offers, Tech happenings around the world, New Release and Sessions with the Authors:

https://discord.bpbonline.com

CHAPTER 6

Concurrency

Introduction

Concurrency is one of Go's most powerful features that lets us write programs that are efficient at performing multiple tasks simultaneously. Concurrency in Go is driven by the lightweight and highly efficient nature of goroutines. In this chapter, we will delve into Go's concurrency model, exploring goroutines, channels, and synchronization mechanisms. Additionally, we will also explore the context package and understand how this package helps manage goroutines.

Structure

This chapter covers the following topics:

- Introduction to concurrency, goroutines and channels
- Buffered versus unbuffered channels
- Select statement
- Synchronization
- Managing concurrency with context package

Objectives

In this chapter, we aim to introduce you to the fundamentals of concurrency in Go. We will explore the efficient use of goroutines for concurrent function execution. You will learn how to use channels for safe communication between goroutines, understand the difference between buffered and unbuffered channels, and explore the select statement for handling multiple channel operations. Additionally, we will delve into the sync package to manage synchronization with tools like **sync.Mutex**, **sync.WaitGroup**, and **sync.Once**. Finally, we will examine the **context** package for managing goroutine lifecycles, enabling cancellation, setting timeouts, and handling request-scoped data.

Introduction to concurrency, goroutines, and channels

Concurrency in Go is built around goroutines. Goroutines are lightweight threads managed by the Go runtime. Unlike traditional threads, goroutines are more efficient and easier to work with, allowing us to run thousands of them concurrently without much overhead.

Goroutine

A goroutine is a function that runs concurrently with other functions. To start a new goroutine, you simply prefix a function call with the **go** keyword.

Here is a simple example:

```go
package main

import (
    "fmt"
    "time"
)
func sayHello() {
    fmt.Println("Hello, Go!")
}
func main() {
    go sayHello()
    time.Sleep(1 * time.Second)
}
```

In the **main** function, **go sayHello()** launches the **sayHello** function as a goroutine. This function runs concurrently with the main function. The **sayHello** function prints **"Hello, Go!"**. The main function waits for a second to ensure the goroutine has time to execute before the program exits.

Characteristics of goroutines

Here are a few characteristics of goroutines:

- **Lightweight**: Goroutines are much lighter than traditional threads. This lets us run many goroutines simultaneously.

- **Managed by Go runtime**: The Go scheduler handles the execution of goroutines, optimizing for performance and resource usage.

- **Stack growth**: Goroutines start with a small stack that grows and shrinks as needed, unlike fixed-size stacks in traditional threads.

Channels

Channels are Go's way of allowing goroutines to communicate with each other. They provide a safe way to send and receive data between goroutines.

Channels are created using the **make** function. Here is how you can create and use a channel:

```
package main

import (
  "fmt"
  "sync"
  "time"
)

func main() {
  var wg sync.WaitGroup // Declare a WaitGroup

  // Create a channel of type int
  messageChannel := make(chan int)
```

```go
wg.Add(2) // We have two goroutines to wait for

// Start a goroutine to send data into the channel
go func() {
  defer wg.Done() // Mark this goroutine
as done when it completes
  for i := 1; i <= 5; i++ {
   fmt.Printf("Sending message %d\n", i)
   messageChannel <- i          // Send the value to
the channel
   time.Sleep(1 * time.Second) // Simulate delay
  }
  close(messageChannel) // Close the channel after
sending all messages
 }()

// Start a goroutine to receive data from the channel
go func() {
  defer wg.Done()
// Mark this goroutine as done when it completes
  for msg := range messageChannel {
// Range over the channel to receive messages
   fmt.Printf("Received message %d\n", msg)
  }
 }()

// Wait for both goroutines to complete
 wg.Wait()
 fmt.Println("Program finished")
}
```

In this example, we create a simple integer unbuffered (we have covered this topic in the next section) channel to enable communication between two goroutines. One goroutine sends numbers (1 to 5) into the channel, pausing for a second between each send. Since the channel is unbuffered, the send operation blocks until the receiver is ready to receive the value. At the same time, the other goroutine receives and prints each message from the channel. After all messages are sent, the channel is closed to signal that no more data will be sent. This makes the receiving goroutine stop listening.

To ensure the main function waits for both goroutines to complete, we use a `sync.WaitGroup`. We call `wg.Add(2)` before starting the goroutines. This indicates that two tasks need to finish. Each goroutine calls `wg.Done()` when it completes which decrements the counter. The `wg.Wait()` call in main blocks execution until the counter reaches zero. This ensures the program only exits after both goroutines have finished.

The output of the program looks like this:

```
Sending message 1
Received message 1
Sending message 2
Received message 2
Sending message 3
Received message 3
Sending message 4
Received message 4
Sending message 5
Received message 5
Program finished
```

Buffered versus unbuffered channels

Channels can be buffered or unbuffered. An unbuffered channel requires both a sender and receiver to be ready at the same time. A buffered channel, on the other hand, allows sending and receiving to occur at different times.

Unbuffered channel

An unbuffered channel provides synchronization between sending and receiving goroutines. In an unbuffered channel, both the sending and receiving operations block until the other side is ready.

In this example, let us see how an unbuffered channel blocks the sending goroutine until a receiver is ready:

```
package main

import (
 "fmt"
 "time"
)

func main() {
 // Create an unbuffered channel
 messageChannel := make(chan string)

 // Sender goroutine
 go func() {
  fmt.Println("Sending message...")
  messageChannel <- "Hello, World!"
// This will block until the receiver is ready
  fmt.Println("Message sent.")
 }()

 // Simulate a delay before receiving
 time.Sleep(2 * time.Second)

 // Receiver in the main goroutine
 fmt.Println("Receiving message...")
 message := <-messageChannel // This will unblock the sender
 fmt.Printf("Message received: %s\n", message)
}
```

Here, the sender goroutine tries to send **"Hello, World!"** into **messageChannel**. Because the channel is unbuffered, the **messageChannel <- "Hello, World!"** operation blocks until a receiver is ready. After a 2-second delay, the main function receives the message, unblocking the sender goroutine.

This program outputs the following:

```
Sending message...
Receiving message...
Message sent.
Message received: Hello, World!
```

Buffered channel

Buffered channels allow for a fixed number of elements to be queued without blocking the sender. The sending goroutine can proceed without waiting for a receiver until the buffer is full. Buffered channels are useful when you want to control communication pacing between goroutines.

Here is an example where a buffered channel allows multiple sends before requiring a receiver:

```go
package main

import (
 "fmt"
 "time"
)

func main() {
 // Create a buffered channel with a capacity of 3
 messageChannel := make(chan string, 3)

 // Sender goroutine
 go func() {
  fmt.Println("Sending message 1")
  messageChannel <- "Message 1" // Won't block
  fmt.Println("Sending message 2")
  messageChannel <- "Message 2" // Won't block
  fmt.Println("Sending message 3")
  messageChannel <- "Message 3" // Won't block
  fmt.Println("All messages sent.")
 }()

 // Simulate a delay before receiving
 time.Sleep(2 * time.Second)

 // Receiver in the main goroutine
 for i := 1; i <= 3; i++ {
  fmt.Printf("Receiving message %d\n", i)
  fmt.Printf("Message received: %s\n", <-messageChannel)
 }
}
```

A buffered channel **messageChannel** is created with a capacity of 3. The sender goroutine sends three messages without waiting for a receiver, as the buffer can hold up to three messages.

The main function receives each message after a delay and prints them in sequence.

The program's output is as follows:

```
Sending message 1
Sending message 2
Sending message 3
All messages sent.
Receiving message 1
Message received: Message 1
Receiving message 2
Message received: Message 2
Receiving message 3
Message received: Message 3
```

Key differences between buffered and unbuffered channels

When working with channels in Go, understanding the distinction between buffered and unbuffered channels is crucial for designing efficient and predictable concurrent systems. Each type of channel serves distinct use cases, offering different levels of synchronization and control over communication flow. Refer to the following table:

Feature	Unbuffered channel	Buffered channel
Blocking behaviour	Sender blocks until a receiver is ready	Sender blocks only when buffer is full
Synchronization	Tight synchronization	Looser synchronization, allows pacing between tasks
Use cases	When exact timing/ sync is needed	When buffering is needed to smooth communication
Examples	Notifications or coordination	Message queuing with controlled flow

Table 6.1: Features of unbuffered and buffered channels

Select statement

The **select** statement lets us wait on multiple channel operations. It blocks until one of its cases can proceed, then executes that case. If multiple channels are ready at the same time, one case is chosen at random.

Here is the basic syntax of the select statement:

```
select {
case <-ch1:
    // Handle channel 1
case msg := <-ch2:
    // Handle channel 2 and use received data
default:
    // Optional: execute if no channels are ready
}
```

Let us say we have two channels sending messages at different intervals. We will use **select** to handle messages from both channels as soon as they arrive. Refer to the following:

```
package main

import (
 "fmt"
 "time"
)

func main() {
 // Create two channels
 ch1 := make(chan string)
 ch2 := make(chan string)

 // Start goroutine to send to ch1
 go func() {
  for {
   ch1 <- "Message from Channel 1"
   time.Sleep(1 * time.Second)
  }
 }()
```

```go
// Start goroutine to send to ch2
go func() {
 for {
  ch2 <- "Message from Channel 2"
  time.Sleep(2 * time.Second)
 }
}()

// Listen to both channels using select
for i := 0; i < 5; i++ {
// Limit to 5 messages for example purposes
 select {
 case msg1 := <-ch1:
  fmt.Println("Received:", msg1)
 case msg2 := <-ch2:
  fmt.Println("Received:", msg2)
 }
}

fmt.Println("Finished listening to channels")
}
```

First, two channels, **ch1** and **ch2**, are created to receive messages. Then, two goroutines send messages to **ch1** and **ch2** every 1 and 2 seconds, respectively. The **select** statement listens to both channels, printing the message received from whichever channel becomes ready first.

Here is the output of the program:

```
Received: Message from Channel 2
Received: Message from Channel 1
Received: Message from Channel 1
Received: Message from Channel 1
Received: Message from Channel 2
Finished listening to channels
```

Synchronization

The **sync** package in Golang provides essential tools for synchronizing goroutines in concurrent programming. Key types in this package, like **sync.Mutex**, **sync.WaitGroup**, and **sync. Once**. They let us coordinate goroutines, protect shared resources, and ensure certain operations only run once. This section provides a guide to the main types in **sync**.

sync.Mutex

A **mutual exclusion** (**Mutex**) is a lock that ensures only one goroutine can access a shared resource at a time. This is used to prevent race conditions when multiple goroutines access or modify the same variable.

Let us understand **sync.Mutex** using this code:

```go
package main

import (
 "fmt"
 "sync"
)

func main() {
 var count int
 var mu sync.Mutex
 var wg sync.WaitGroup

 for i := 0; i < 5; i++ {
  wg.Add(1)
  go func() {
   defer wg.Done()
   mu.Lock() // Lock before accessing resource
   fmt.Printf("Locking Mutex - Goroutine %d\n", i)
   count++ // Safe increment
   fmt.Printf("Unlocking Mutex - Goroutine %d\n", i)
   mu.Unlock() // Unlock after accessing resource
  }()
 }

 wg.Wait()
 fmt.Println("Final Count:", count)
}
```

In this code, **mu.Lock()** prevents other goroutines from accessing count until **mu.Unlock()** is called.

The **count++** operation is thread-safe, ensuring accurate results.

The output is as follows:

```
Locking Mutex - Goroutine 4
Unlocking Mutex - Goroutine 4
Locking Mutex - Goroutine 1
Unlocking Mutex - Goroutine 1
Locking Mutex - Goroutine 0
Unlocking Mutex - Goroutine 0
Locking Mutex - Goroutine 2
Unlocking Mutex - Goroutine 2
Locking Mutex - Goroutine 3
Unlocking Mutex - Goroutine 3
Final Count: 5
```

sync.WaitGroup

WaitGroup is used to wait for a collection of goroutines to finish executing. It helps us wait for a group of goroutines to finish before proceeding. The use of **WaitGroup** allows the program to wait for all goroutines without needing arbitrary delays.

It provides **Add**, **Done**, and **Wait** methods for adding goroutines, marking them as done, and blocking until all are complete. Refer to the following code:

```
package main

import (
 "fmt"
 "sync"
)

func worker(id int, wg *sync.WaitGroup) {
 defer wg.Done()
 fmt.Printf("Worker %d starting\n", id)
 // Simulate work
```

```
  fmt.Printf("Worker %d done\n", id)
}

func main() {
  var wg sync.WaitGroup

  for i := 1; i <= 3; i++ {
    wg.Add(1)
    go worker(i, &wg)
  }

  wg.Wait()
  fmt.Printf("Exiting main")
}
```

Here, we have a **worker** function that takes an ID and a pointer to a **WaitGroup**. Each worker prints a message when it starts and completes, simulating some work in between. In main, a **WaitGroup (wg)** is created to track the completion of multiple goroutines. For each worker, **wg.Add(1)** increments the counter to indicate a new goroutine that must complete. Each worker goroutine calls **wg.Done()** when it finishes, decrementing the counter. Finally, **wg.Wait()** blocks the **main** function until all worker goroutines have called **Done**, ensuring that the program only exits after all goroutines complete their tasks.

sync.Once

sync.Once ensures a function or block of code is executed only once, even when called from multiple goroutines. This is useful for one-time initialization tasks. Refer to the following:

```
package main

import (
  "fmt"
  "sync"
)

func main() {
  var once sync.Once
```

```go
var wg sync.WaitGroup

initialize := func() {
 fmt.Println("Initializing resources")
}

for i := 1; i <= 3; i++ {
 wg.Add(1)
 go func(id int) {
  defer wg.Done()
  once.Do(initialize) // Ensures initialize runs only once
  fmt.Printf("Goroutine %d completed\n", id)
 }(i)
}

wg.Wait()
}
```

In the above code, **once.Do(initialize)** guarantees that initialize is called only once, regardless of how many goroutines attempt to call it.

The program's output looks as follows:

```
Initializing resources
Goroutine 3 completed
Goroutine 2 completed
Goroutine 1 completed
```

Managing concurrency with context package

The **context** package provides a way to manage deadlines, cancellation signals, and other request-scoped values across API boundaries and between processes.

The **context** package helps us manage concurrency, especially when working with long-running or potentially cancellable tasks in goroutines. It allows us to control the lifecycle of goroutines, handle deadlines, and propagate cancellation signals across multiple goroutines.

Introduction to context

A `context.Context` is a lightweight, immutable data structure that holds cancellation, deadlines, and request-scoped values. It is used to control goroutines and handle cross-goroutine communication. Key functions provided by the package include `context.Background()`, `context.WithCancel()`, `context.WithDeadline()`, and `context.WithTimeout()`.

Creating a base context

The base `context.Background()` or `context.TODO()` provides an initial context. Typically, `context.Background()` is used as the root context from which you can derive other contexts.

Base context can be assigned to a variable like this:

```
ctx := context.Background() // Base context
```

context.WithCancel

`context.WithCancel` creates a new context that can be canceled, which lets us stop any goroutines using it.

In the following code, we cancel a long-running task using context cancellation:

```
package main

import (
 "context"
 "fmt"
 "time"
)

func main() {
 // Create a cancellable context
 ctx, cancel := context.WithCancel(context.Background())
 defer cancel()

 // Launch a goroutine with the context
 go func() {
  for {
```

```
    select {
    case <-ctx.Done():
     fmt.Println("Goroutine stopped")
     return
    default:
     fmt.Println("Goroutine running...")
     time.Sleep(500 * time.Millisecond)
    }
  }
 }()

 time.Sleep(2 * time.Second)
 // Allow the goroutine to run for a bit
 cancel()                    // Cancel the context
 time.Sleep(1 * time.Second)  // Wait for the final message
}
```

Here, **context.WithCancel** creates a context **ctx** and a **cancel** function. The goroutine monitors **ctx.Done()** in a **select** block. When **cancel()** is called, **ctx.Done()** is triggered, and the goroutine stops.

Here is the output of the program:

```
Goroutine running...
Goroutine running...
Goroutine running...
Goroutine running...
Goroutine stopped
```

context.WithTimeout

context.WithTimeout sets a time limit for how long a context remains active. If the deadline is reached, the context is canceled automatically. We can use **context.WithTimeout** to set limits on time-consuming tasks like API calls or database queries.

Let us look at an example:

```
package main

import (
```

```
"context"
"fmt"
"time"
)

func main() {
// Create a context with a 2-second timeout
ctx, cancel := context.WithTimeout(context.Background(),
2*time.Second)
defer cancel()

// Launch a task that will check for context timeout
go func() {
  select {
  case <-ctx.Done():
   fmt.Println("Timeout reached:", ctx.Err())
   return
  case <-time.After(3 * time.Second):
// Simulate long-running task
   fmt.Println("Task completed")
  }
}()

time.Sleep(3 * time.Second) // Wait to observe the output
}
```

In the above code, **context.WithTimeout** automatically cancels **ctx** after 2 seconds. The goroutine has a sleep of 3 seconds. Since the task does not complete before the timeout of 2 seconds, the context **ctx** gets canceled. This terminates the goroutines.

context.WithValue

context.WithValue attaches data to a context. This is helpful for passing request-scoped information, like user IDs or authorization tokens, to child goroutines. Refer to the following:

```
package main

import (
  "context"
  "fmt"
```

```
)

func main() {
 // Create a context with a key-value pair
 ctx := context.WithValue(context.
Background(), "userID", 42)

 // Start a goroutine that accesses the context value
 go func(ctx context.Context) {
  userID := ctx.Value("userID")
  fmt.Println("UserID from context:», userID)
 }(ctx)
}
```

In this code, **context.WithValue** attaches a **userID** value to **ctx**. The goroutine retrieves and uses **userID** from **ctx**.

Conclusion

We explored the fundamental techniques to utilize concurrency in Go. We covered how to harness goroutines for parallel task execution and how channels facilitate safe communication between them. We started with the basics of channel types—buffered and unbuffered—and saw how they manage data flow and synchronization. We then introduced the select statement to handle multiple channels concurrently. We examined the sync package, and explored sync.Mutex, sync.WaitGroup, and sync. Once for managing shared resources. Finally, we dove into the context package, which offers critical support for managing goroutine lifecycles with cancellations, timeouts, and data sharing. With these tools, you are now equipped with a robust foundation to create efficient, responsive concurrent applications in Go.

In the following chapter, we will explore structs, struct embedding for creating composite structures, overriding embedded fields, and defining methods to attach behavior to structs. The chapter will also cover interfaces, their implementation, type assertion and type switch statement.

CHAPTER 7

Structs, Methods, and Interfaces

Introduction

Structs are a foundational feature in Go that allow developers to group related data into cohesive units. Unlike arrays and slices, which store elements of a single type, structs can hold fields of differing types. In this chapter, we will explore how to define, instantiate, and use structs in Go. We will delve into advanced features like struct embedding for creating composite structures, overriding embedded fields, and defining methods to attach behavior to structs, enabling more organized and maintainable code. We will also cover interfaces, their implementation, type assertion and type switch statement.

Structure

This chapter covers the following topics:

- Structs
- Structs with embedded fields
- Methods
- Method receivers: Value vs. pointer
- Method chaining
- Interfaces

- Type assertion
- Type switch

Objectives

By the end of this chapter, you will understand what structs are and how they differ from other Go types. You will learn to define structs with fields of varying types, instantiate them with initial values, and explore how Go handles zero values for struct fields to simplify initialization. Additionally, you will gain insights into struct embedding for creating composite types and reusing code, while understanding how to override embedded fields to customize behavior. The chapter will also guide you in defining and using methods to encapsulate behavior within structs, distinguish between value and pointer receivers for methods, and learn their appropriate use cases. You will also explore method chaining to create fluent and intuitive interfaces. Additionally, you will learn about interfaces, their implementation, type assertion and type switch.

Structs

Structs in Golang are user-defined types that allow us to group related data together. They form a cohesive unit that represents an entity or concept in our application. Structs differ from other collection types like arrays and slices in Go. While arrays and slices store elements of a single type, structs can contain fields of differing types, making them versatile for modeling real-world entities.

In many ways, structs in Go function similarly to dictionaries in Python or structs in C, providing a way to organize related data under a single type.

Imagine you are building an HR management system. Each employee has attributes such as their first name, last name, and age. Using a **struct**, you can encapsulate these attributes within a single type:

```go
type Employee struct {
```

```
   FirstName string
   LastName  string
   Age       int
}
```

This encapsulation eliminates the need for managing separate variables for each attribute, resulting in cleaner and more maintainable code.

Structs are particularly useful in application development for modeling complex data structures, such as users, products, or orders.

Defining structs

Defining a struct in Go is straightforward. You use the **type** keyword followed by the struct name and the **struct** keyword. Inside the curly braces **{}**, you define the fields and their types.

Here is a simple example of a **Person** struct:

```
type Person struct {
    Name string
    Age  int
}
```

In this example, the **Person** struct has two fields:

- **Name**: A string representing the person's name.
- **Age**: An integer representing the person's age.

The fields of a **struct** can be of any data type, including other structs or slices.

Here is an example of a struct that includes a slice, a function, and a Boolean field:

```
type Employee struct {
    Name     string
    Age      int
    Skills   []string  // Slice of strings
    IsActive bool      // Boolean field
    Promote  func()    // Function field
}
```

This struct allows us to represent an employee with a set of skills, an active status, and even a function that can perform an action.

Instantiating and using structs

To create an instance of a struct, you can use the struct literal syntax. Here is how you can instantiate and use the **Person** struct:

```
person := Person{Name: "Alice", Age: 30}
fmt.Println(person.Name) // Output: Alice
fmt.Println(person.Age)  // Output: 30
```

Here, the **person** variable holds an instance of the **Person** struct with fields initialized to specific values.

You can also modify the fields of a struct after it has been instantiated:

```
person.Age = 31
fmt.Println(person.Age) // Output: 31
```

Let us create an instance of **Employee**:

```
employee := Employee{
    Name:     "Bob",
    Age:      28,
    Skills:   []string{"Go", "Docker", "Kubernetes"},
    IsActive: true,
    Promote: func() {
        fmt.Println("Employee promoted!")
    },
}
```

```
fmt.Println(employee.Name)        // Output: Bob
fmt.Println(employee.Skills[0])   // Output: Go
fmt.Println(employee.IsActive)    // Output: true
employee.Promote()    // Output: Employee promoted!
```

In this example, an **Employee** struct is instantiated with fields of different types, including a slice (**Skills**), a Boolean (**IsActive**), and a function (**Promote**). The **struct** stores details about an employee named **Bob**, who has expertise in Go, Docker, and Kubernetes and is currently active. When the **Promote** function is called, it prints a message indicating that the **employee** has been promoted, demonstrating how structs can encapsulate both data and behavior.

Using zero values

When a struct is instantiated without initializing fields, Go assigns default zero values to each field. For example:

```
var emptyPerson Person
fmt.Println(emptyPerson.Name) // Output: ""
fmt.Println(emptyPerson.Age)  // Output: 0
```

For more complex structs like the **Employee** struct that we created earlier, zero values look like this:

```
var newEmployee Employee
fmt.Println(newEmployee.Skills)   // Output: []
fmt.Println(newEmployee.IsActive) // Output: false
fmt.Println(newEmployee.Promote)  // Output: <nil>
```

This behavior ensures structs are always initialized safely.

Ways to initialize a struct

In Go, you can initialize a struct in multiple ways:

Using struct literalusing named fields

This is the most common and recommended way to initialize a struct, as it explicitly assigns values to specific fields, improving readability.

Here is an example of using named fields.

```
person := Person{Name: "Alice", Age: 30}
```

Using struct literal using positional fields

You can also initialize a struct by providing values in the same order as the struct fields as shown:

```
person := Person{"Alice", 30}
```

However, this approach can be error-prone, especially if the struct has many fields.

Using the new keyword

The new keyword creates a zero-initialized struct and returns a pointer to it. You can then modify its fields as needed. Here is an example:

```
person := new(Person)
person.Name = "Alice"
person.Age = 30
```

Using a struct pointer with the & operator

Instead of using the new keyword, you can create a struct instance using the **&** operator. This approach directly returns a pointer to the newly created struct, allowing efficient memory usage and easier modification without creating copies.

Here is an example:

```
person := &Person{Name: "Alice", Age: 30}
```

In this case, **person** is a pointer to a **Person** struct. Since Go automatically dereferences struct pointers when accessing fields, you do not need to use **(*person).Name**—you can simply write **person.Name**.

Immutable structs in Go

Go does not support fully immutable structs like const struct in some languages, but you can achieve immutability by defining struct fields with lowercase names. These fields become inaccessible outside the package. You can provide getter methods to allow controlled access.

Here is an example:

```
type Employee struct {
    name string  // unexported field
}

func NewEmployee(name string) Employee {
    return Employee{name: name}
}

func (e Employee) GetName() string {
```

```
    return e.name
}
```

In this approach, once an **Employee** instance is created, its **name** field cannot be modified directly. To retrive the **name** field, one has to use **GetName** function. If you which to create a new **Employess**, you need to use the **NewEmployee** function.

Structs with embedded fields

Struct embedding allows us to include one struct within another. Embedding inherits the fields of the nested struct into the parent struct.

This promotes code reuse and organization by enabling you to compose complex data structures. By embedding one struct into another, you can create complex structures that inherit the fields of the embedded struct.

Consider a **Student** struct that embeds the **Person** struct:

```
type Student struct {
    Person
    StudentID string
}
```

With embedding, the **Student** struct inherits the fields of the **Person** struct, allowing us to access them directly:

```
student := Student{
    Person:    Person{Name: "Bob", Age: 20},
    StudentID: "S1234",
}
fmt.Println(student.Name)      // Output: Bob
fmt.Println(student.StudentID) // Output: S1234
```

Overriding embedded fields

If the embedding struct defines a field with the same name as an embedded field, the embedding struct's field takes precedence:

```
type Graduate struct {
    Person
    Degree string
```

```
    Name    string // Overrides Person.Name
}
graduate := Graduate{
    Person: Person{Name: "Alice", Age: 25},
    Degree: "Master's",
    Name:    "Dr. Alice",
}
fmt.Println(graduate.Name)   // Output: Dr. Alice
fmt.Println(graduate.Person.Name) // Output: Alice
```

This feature enables you to customize the behavior of embedded structs without losing access to their original fields.

Methods

In Go, methods are functions with an attached receiver that specifies the type of the method is associated with. This feature allows you to define behavior directly tied to a type, such as a struct. By associating methods with types, Go facilitates a structured approach to encapsulating data and its related functionality.

Methods are fundamental in Go's approach to object-oriented programming, despite Go not having traditional classes. They enable developers to define actions that types can perform, making it easier to model real-world behavior.

Defining methods on structs

To define a method, you specify the receiver type between the **func** keyword and the method name. Here is how you can add a **Greet** method to the **Person** struct:

```
type Person struct {
    Name string
    Age  int
}

// Method with a value receiver
func (p Person) Greet() {
    fmt.Printf("Hello, my name is %s.\n", p.Name)
}
```

In this example, **p** is the receiver of type **Person**. You can call the **Greet** method on any instance of **Person**:

```
person := Person{Name: "Alice", Age: 30}
person.Greet() // Output: Hello, my name is Alice.
```

This method demonstrates how behavior (greeting) can be tied directly to data (Person), making the code more cohesive and readable.

Method receivers: Value vs. pointer

When defining methods, you can choose between value and pointer receivers. A value receiver operates on a copy of the struct, while a pointer receiver operates on the original struct, allowing you to modify its fields.

Value receivers

A value receiver gets a copy of the struct. Use value receivers when:

- The method does not need to modify the struct.
- The struct is small, and copying it is inexpensive.

Let us look at the following example:

```
func (p Person) DisplayAge() {
    fmt.Printf("I am %d years old.\n", p.Age)
}

person := Person{Name: "Alice", Age: 30}
person.DisplayAge() // Output: I am 30 years old.
```

Here, changes to **p** within the method will not affect the original **Person** instance.

Pointer receivers

A pointer receiver gets a reference to the original struct, enabling methods to modify its fields. Use pointer receivers when:

- The method needs to modify the struct.
- The struct is large, and passing a pointer avoids expensive copying.

Here is an example of pointer receiver:

```go
func (p *Person) IncrementAge() {
    p.Age++
}

person := Person{Name: "Alice", Age: 30}
person.IncrementAge()
fmt.Println(person.Age) // Output: 31
```

The **IncrementAge** method modifies the **Age** field of the original **Person** instance.

Method chaining

Method chaining is a technique that allows you to call multiple methods in a single statement, creating a fluent interface. This is particularly useful in builder patterns.

Here is an example of method chaining:

```go
type Builder struct {
    value int
}

func (b *Builder) Add(v int) *Builder {
    b.value += v
    return b
}

func (b *Builder) Multiply(v int) *Builder {
    b.value *= v
    return b
}

builder := &Builder{}
result := builder.Add(5).Multiply(2).value
fmt.Println(result) // Output: 10
```

In this example, there are a couple of key concepts that we should look at:

- **Returning the receiver**: Each method returns the pointer to the instance (***Builder**), enabling subsequent method calls.

- **Fluent interface**: The code reads naturally as a sequence of operations.

Interfaces

Interfaces in Go provide a way to define and enforce behavior through a set of method signatures. Unlike in some other languages, Go interfaces are **implicit**. This means a type satisfies an interface simply by implementing its methods, without explicit declarations. This feature enables polymorphism, where different types can be treated uniformly as long as they implement the required methods.

Interfaces are a cornerstone of Go's design philosophy, promoting loosely coupled and highly extensible code.

Defining and implementing interfaces

To define an interface, use the **type** keyword followed by the interface name and the **interface** keyword. Here is an example of a **Speaker** interface:

```
type Speaker interface {
    Speak() string
}
```

Here, any type that implements the **Speak** method satisfies the **Speaker** interface.

The following is an example where a **Dog** type implements the **Speaker** interface:

```
type Dog struct{}

func (d Dog) Speak() string {
    return "Woof!"
}

var s Speaker = Dog{}
fmt.Println(s.Speak()) // Output: Woof!
```

There are a few key points to note here:

- **Implicit satisfaction**: The **Dog** struct satisfies the **Speaker** interface simply because it implements the **Speak** method.

- **Polymorphism in action**: You can assign an instance of **Dog** to a variable of type **Speaker**, demonstrating polymorphism.

Interface composition

Interface composition allows you to create new interfaces by combining existing ones. This promotes modularity and code reuse.

Here is an example of composing interfaces:

```
type Mover interface {
    Move()
}

type Human interface {
    Speaker
    Mover
}
```

In this example, the **Human** interface embeds both **Speaker** and **Mover**, meaning any type that satisfies **Human** must implement the methods of both interfaces.

Let us take a look at its usage:

```
type Athlete struct{}

func (a Athlete) Speak() string {
    return "I am an athlete."
}

func (a Athlete) Move() {
    fmt.Println("Running...")
}

var h Human = Athlete{}
fmt.Println(h.Speak()) // Output: I am an athlete.
h.Move()               // Output: Running...
```

Type assertion

Type assertion is used to extract the underlying value of an interface. Since interfaces can hold values of any type, type assertion becomes essential when you need to access the underlying concrete type safely. It allows you to access the concrete type that implements the interface:

```
var i interface{} = 42
n, ok := i.(int)
if ok {
    fmt.Println(n) // Output: 42
} else {
    fmt.Println("Type assertion failed.")
}
```

In the preceding code, if **i** holds a value of type **int**, the assertion succeeds, and **ok** is true.

Type switch

A **type** switch is a powerful construct for handling multiple possible concrete types in a type-safe manner. It evaluates an interface value's underlying type and executes different code depending on the type.

Let us take an example:

```
var i interface{} = "hello"

switch v := i.(type) {
case int:
    fmt.Printf("Integer: %d\n", v)
case string:
    fmt.Printf("String: %s\n", v)
default:
    fmt.Println("Unknown type")
}
```

In the preceding code, the **type** keyword in a type switch represents the underlying type of the interface. Each **case** handles a specific type. The **default** clause handles cases where none of the specified types match.

Practical applications

Here are a few practical applications of interfaces:

- **Polymorphism**: Enable functions to accept different types while operating on common behavior.

- **Mocking in tests**: Interfaces allow you to mock dependencies for testing purposes.

- **Standardized APIs**: Many Go packages, such as `io.Reader` and `io.Writer`, leverage interfaces to provide consistent APIs.

- **Extensibility**: Using interfaces ensures that adding new types with shared behavior does not require modifying existing code.

Conclusion

In this chapter, we explored the power and flexibility of structs in Go. We started by understanding how structs group related data into a single type, making them ideal for modeling real-world entities. We learned to define and instantiate structs, initialize fields, and modify them after creation. We also examined Go's default handling of zero values.

Moving into more advanced concepts, we introduced struct embedding to create composite types. We explored how to override embedded fields for customization while retaining access to the original struct's fields. Methods added functionality to structs, enabling us to attach behavior directly to types. We differentiated between value and pointer receivers.

We also delved into interfaces. Interfaces enable polymorphism by allowing different types to be treated uniformly as long as they implement the required methods. We covered how to define and implement interfaces and explored interface composition. Finally, we examined type assertions and type switches to work with interface values effectively.

By mastering these techniques, you are now equipped to leverage structs to build robust, maintainable, and reusable components in your Go applications.

CHAPTER 8

Working with JSON and HTTP

Introduction

In modern web development, handling data efficiently and building robust HTTP servers are fundamental skills. Go's standard library provides powerful tools to achieve this. The net/http package creates web servers, and the encoding/json package seamlessly works with JSON data. This chapter dives into these essential components, offering a comprehensive guide to building web applications in Go. From encoding and decoding JSON to implementing middleware and context handling, you will learn how to create efficient and maintainable web servers that cater to dynamic client requirements.

Structure

This chapter covers the following topics:

- Introduction to JSON in Go
- Encoding and decoding JSON
- Building a simple web server
- Handling JSON in HTTP requests and responses
- Routing and handling HTTP requests
- Middleware and context in HTTP servers

Objectives

By the end of this chapter, you will have a solid understanding of how to work with JSON data using Go's **encoding/json** package, enabling you to seamlessly encode and decode JSON for interacting with **application programming interfaces (APIs)** and data sources. You will learn to handle JSON effectively in HTTP requests and responses, facilitating smooth data exchange between clients and servers. Additionally, you will gain the skills to build a simple web server using the **net/http** package, implement routing to manage different HTTP methods and paths, and enhance your server with middleware for tasks like logging and authentication. Lastly, you will explore how to use Go's **context** package to handle request cancellations, deadlines, and request-scoped data, ensuring efficient and reliable resource management in your web applications.

Introduction to JSON in Go

JavaScript Object Notation (JSON) is a popular data interchange format due to its human-readable structure and ease of use. It is widely used in web development, APIs, and microservices to exchange data. JSON represents data as key-value pairs, making it easy to parse and generate in different programming languages.

The **encoding/json** package, part of the standard library, facilitates JSON handling in Go. This package provides powerful and flexible functionality for encoding Go data structures into JSON and decoding JSON data back into Go data structures. Understanding how to effectively work with JSON in Go is essential, whether you are working with RESTful APIs, interacting with third-party services, or storing configuration data.

Encoding and decoding JSON

The process of handling JSON in Go involves two main operations: **encoding** Go data into JSON and **decoding** JSON data into Go data structures. Let us explore these in detail.

Encoding JSON

Encoding data into JSON is the process of converting Go data structures into a JSON-encoded format, typically represented as a **[ ]byte**. This can be achieved using the **json.Marshal** function.

Here is an example:

```
package main

import (
    "encoding/json"
    "fmt"
)

type Person struct {
    Name string `json:"name"`
    Age  int    `json:"age"`
}

func main() {
    p := Person{Name: "Alice", Age: 30}
    jsonData, err := json.Marshal(p)
    if err != nil {
        fmt.Println("Error encoding JSON:", err)
        return
    }
    fmt.Println(string(jsonData))
}
```

Here, the **Person** struct is defined with two fields, **Name** and **Age**, each annotated with JSON tags (**json:"name"** and **json:"age"**) that specify the keys to use when marshaling the struct to JSON. In the **main** function, an instance of **Person** is created. The **json.Marshal** function is used to convert this struct into a JSON-formatted byte slice. If successful, the JSON byte slice is converted to a string and printed.

Here is the output of the program:

```
{"name":"Alice","age":30}
```

Tips for encoding JSON

Let us explore how to encode Go structs into JSON effectively, leveraging features like struct tags for customization, **omitempty** for optional fields, and robust error handling to ensure reliability and clarity in your JSON outputs:

- **Utilize struct tags for customization**: Struct tags allow you to control how Go struct fields are represented in the JSON output. For example, by specifying a JSON key in the struct tag, you can ensure the field name in the JSON matches your desired format, even if the Go field name is different. This is useful for adhering to specific JSON API requirements or conventions. Let us look at an example:

```go
type Person struct {
    Name string `json:"full_name"`
}
```

This ensures the field **Name** is encoded as **full_name** in JSON.

- **Handle optional or omitted fields**: Adding **omitempty** in struct tags prevents fields with zero values (e.g., **0** for integers, **""** for strings, or **nil** for pointers) from being included in the JSON output. This keeps the JSON payload concise and avoids transmitting unnecessary data. For instance:

```go
type Person struct {
    Age int `json:"age,omitempty"`
}
```

If **Age** is **0**, the resulting JSON will not include the **age** field.

- **Error handling is crucial**: Always handle errors returned by **json.Marshal** or other JSON-related functions to ensure robustness. Encoding can fail due to invalid data types, unsupported structures, or memory constraints. By checking for errors, we can gracefully handle these edge cases instead of encountering runtime failures. Let us look at an example:

```go
jsonData, err := json.Marshal(p)
if err != nil {
    fmt.Println("Error encoding JSON:", err)
```

```
    return
    }
    fmt.Println(string(jsonData))
```

Decoding JSON

Decoding JSON involves parsing a JSON string (or byte slice) into a Go data structure. This is done using the **json.Unmarshal** function.

Here is an example:

```
package main

import (
    "encoding/json"
    "fmt"
)

type Person struct {
    Name string `json:"name"`
    Age  int    `json:"age"`
}

func main() {
    // JSON string
    jsonData := `{"name":"Alice","age":30}`

    // Define a variable to hold the decoded data
    var p Person

    // Decode JSON into the Go struct
    err := json.Unmarshal([]byte(jsonData), &p)
    if err != nil {
        fmt.Println("Error decoding JSON:", err)
        return
    }

    // Print the decoded struct
    fmt.Printf("Name: %s, Age: %d\n", p.Name, p.Age)
}
```

In this code, the **Person** struct is defined with two fields similar to the previous section. In the **main** function, a JSON string (**jsonData**) containing information about a person is defined. The **json.Unmarshal** function is used to parse this JSON string into an instance of the **Person** struct (**p**). The JSON string is first converted into a **byte slice**, which **json.Unmarshal** requires. If the decoding succeeds, the values are mapped to the struct fields, and the data is printed.

The output of the program is as follows:

```
Name: Alice, Age: 30
```

Error scenarios and types

Let us look at the types of errors **json** unmarshalling can throw. If the JSON is incorrect, **json.Unmarshal** returns an error of type ***json.SyntaxError** or ***json.UnmarshalTypeError**, depending on the issue. Here are common cases:

- **Syntax error:** This error occurs when the JSON string is malformed, such as missing quotes, brackets, or commas.

  Here is an example of syntax error:

  ```
  jsonData := `{"name":"Alice","age":30,}`
  var p Person

  err := json.Unmarshal([]byte(jsonData), &p)
  if err != nil {
      fmt.Println("Error decoding JSON:", err)
      fmt.Println("Error type:", reflect.TypeOf(err))
  }
  ```

  In the above code, an extra comma after the **age** field causes a syntax error. This causes **json.Unmarshal** to return a ***json.SyntaxError** indicating an unexpected character. We are also printing the type of error using the **reflect** package. This is evident in the output of the program:

  ```
  Error decoding JSON: *json.SyntaxError
  Error type: *json.SyntaxError
  ```

- **Type mismatch error:** A type mismatch error occurs when the JSON value type does not match the expected Go struct field type.

  In the following example, the **age** field is provided as a string (**"thirty"**), while the Go struct expects an integer.

```
jsonData := `{"name":"Alice","age":"thirty"}`
var p Person

err := json.Unmarshal([]byte(jsonData), &p)
if err != nil {
    fmt.Println("Error decoding JSON:", err)
    fmt.Println("Error type:", reflect.TypeOf(err))
}
```

Since **age** is provided as a string (**"thirty"**), **json. Unmarshal** raises a ***json.UnmarshalTypeError**, indicating that the value cannot be converted into the expected int type. The output of the program looks like this:

```
Error decoding JSON: json: cannot unmarshal string
into Go struct field Person.age of type int
Error type: *json.UnmarshalTypeError
```

- **Unknown fields**: An unknown field error occurs when the JSON contains keys not defined in the target Go struct. By default, Go ignores unknown fields, but using **json.Decoder.DisallowUnknownFields()** forces an error when such fields are encountered.

  In the following example, the JSON includes an additional **"gender"** field, which is not defined in the **Person** struct:

```
jsonData := `{"name":"Alice","age":30,
"gender":"female"}`
var p Person

dec := json.NewDecoder(strings.NewReader(jsonData))
dec.DisallowUnknownFields()

err := dec.Decode(&p)
if err != nil {
  fmt.Println("Error decoding JSON:", err)
  fmt.Println("Error type:", reflect.TypeOf(err))
}
```

The **gender** field is not defined in the **Person** struct. Since **json. Decoder.DisallowUnknownFields()** is used, **json.Unmarshal** returns a ***errors.errorString** error, preventing the decoding process from succeeding.

Here is the output of the program:

```
Error decoding JSON: json: unknown field "gender"
Error type: *errors.errorString
```

Tips for decoding JSON

In this section, we will explore the best practices and techniques for decoding JSON efficiently, ensuring data integrity, and handling dynamic or nested structures with ease:

- **Match Go structs to JSON schema**: When decoding JSON into a struct, ensure that the structure of the Go struct matches the schema of the JSON data. Field names in the JSON must align with the JSON tags or field names in the Go struct. Any mismatch can lead to missing data or errors. If the JSON contains additional fields not present in the struct, they will be ignored during decoding.

- **Always check for errors**: Decoding can fail for various reasons, such as invalid JSON format, unexpected data types, or missing required fields. Always check the error returned by **json.Unmarshal** to handle these situations gracefully.

- **Handle dynamic JSON**: For JSON structures that are dynamic or not fully known at compile time, use a map of string keys to **interface{}** values (**map[string] interface{}**) to decode the data. This allows you to work with the JSON content in a flexible, key-value format without predefining a struct. Let us look at an example:

```
var data map[string]interface{}
err := json.Unmarshal([]byte(jsonData), &data)
if err != nil {
    fmt.Println("Error decoding JSON:", err)
    return
}
fmt.Println(data["name"])
```

While this approach is versatile, keep in mind that you may need to perform type assertions to access specific fields since **interface{}** can hold any type.

- **Decode into slices for arrays**: If the JSON contains an array, decode it into a slice of the appropriate type. For example:

```
jsonArray := `[{"name":"Alice","age":30},
{"name":"Bob","age":25}]`
var people []Person
err := json.Unmarshal([]byte(jsonArray), &people)
if err != nil {
    fmt.Println("Error decoding JSON array:", err)
    return
}
fmt.Println(people)
```

Building a simple web server

Creating a web server in Go is remarkably simple with the **net/http** package. The **net/http** package is a powerful tool for building web servers in Go. It provides essential components like **http.Handler**, **http.Request**, and **http.ResponseWriter** to handle HTTP requests and responses.

To create a web server, you define HTTP handlers and start the server using **http.ListenAndServe**.

```
package main

import (
    "fmt"
    "net/http"
)

func helloHandler(w http.ResponseWriter, r *http.
Request) {
    fmt.Fprintln(w, "Hello, World!")
}
func main() {
    http.HandleFunc("/hello", helloHandler)
    http.ListenAndServe(":8080", nil)
}
```

The code sets up a simple HTTP server to respond with a plain text message. The **helloHandler** function handles requests to the **/hello** endpoint. When this endpoint is accessed, the

function writes **"Hello, World!"** to the HTTP response using
fmt.Fprintln. The main function maps the **/hello** route to the
helloHandler function using **http.HandleFunc**. It then starts
the server on port 8080 with **http.ListenAndServe**.

Handling JSON in HTTP requests and responses

When building web applications, you often need to handle JSON
data in HTTP requests and responses. The **net/http** package
provides tools to facilitate this process.

Handling JSON requests

To handle JSON requests, we need to read the request body and
decode the JSON data into a Go struct. This is common in RESTful
APIs where clients send data in JSON format.

Here is how you can handle a POST request with a JSON payload:

```go
package main

import (
    "encoding/json"
    "fmt"
    "net/http"
)

type Person struct {
    Name string `json:"name"`
    Age  int    `json:"age"`
}

func personHandler(w http.ResponseWriter, r *http.Request) {
    var person Person
    err := json.NewDecoder(r.Body).Decode(&person)
    if err != nil {
        http.Error(w, "Invalid JSON", http.StatusBadRequest)
        return
    }
    fmt.Fprintf(w, "Received: %s, Age: %d\n", person.Name, person.Age)
}
```

```go
func main() {
    http.HandleFunc("/person", personHandler)
    http.ListenAndServe(":8080", nil)
}
```

This code defines a **Person** struct with fields **Name** and **Age**, annotated with JSON tags for parsing. The **personHandler** function processes POST requests to the **/person** endpoint. It uses **json.NewDecoder** to parse the JSON payload from the request body into a **Person** struct. If the payload is invalid, it responds with an **HTTP 400 Bad Request** error. Otherwise, it extracts the **Name** and **Age** fields from the parsed struct and writes a response to the client. The **main** function sets up the **/person** endpoint using **http.HandleFunc** and starts the server on port **8080**. This structure efficiently handles JSON payloads, ensuring proper validation and error handling.

Sending JSON responses

Similarly, we can send JSON data in HTTP responses. To send JSON responses, we encode the Go struct into JSON and write it to the response writer. This is useful for returning structured data to clients:

```go
package main
import (
    "encoding/json"
    "net/http"
)

type Person struct {
    Name string `json:"name"`
    Age  int    `json:"age"`
}

func personHandler(w http.ResponseWriter, r *http.Request) {
    person := Person{Name: "Alice", Age: 30}
    w.Header().Set("Content-Type", "application/json")
    json.NewEncoder(w).Encode(person)
}

func main() {
```

```
    http.HandleFunc("/person", personHandler)
    http.ListenAndServe(":8080", nil)
}
```

Here, we define the same **Person** struct. The **personHandler** function handles requests to the **/person** endpoint. It creates a **Person** instance with predefined values and sets the **Content-Type** header to **application/json** to indicate a JSON response. The **json.NewEncoder** function is then used to encode the **Person** struct as a JSON object and write it to the HTTP response. This structure ensures the server properly formats and sends JSON responses to clients.

Routing and handling HTTP requests

Routing is essential for directing HTTP requests to the appropriate handlers. The **net/http** package provides basic routing capabilities.

You can use **http.HandleFunc** to map URL paths to handler functions.

We will break this down into the following sections.

Basic routing with query parameters

The following example showcases how to handle routes with query parameters in an HTTP server. Query parameters allow clients to send additional data in the URL, enabling dynamic responses. By leveraging **r.URL.Query()**, the server can extract these parameters and personalize the response.

```
package main

import (
 "fmt"
 "net/http"
)

func greetHandler(w http.ResponseWriter, r *http.
Request) {
 name := r.URL.Query().Get("name")
```

```
if name == "" {
 name = "World"
 }
 fmt.Fprintf(w, "Hello, %s!", name)
}
func main() {
 http.HandleFunc("/greet", greetHandler)
 http.ListenAndServe(":8080", nil)
}
```

This example defines a single route **/greet**. The handler **greetHandler** extracts the name query parameter from the URL (e.g., **/greet?name=John**). If name is not provided, it defaults to **"World"**. The response is dynamically generated using **fmt. Fprintf**.

Handling different HTTP methods

In this example, the focus is on distinguishing and responding to different HTTP methods, such as GET and POST. The **net/ http** package provides a straightforward way to handle method-specific behavior, demonstrating how to create versatile routes that adapt to client requests.

```
package main

import (
 "fmt"
 "net/http"
)
func methodHandler(w http.ResponseWriter, r *http.
Request) {
 switch r.Method {
 case http.MethodGet:
  fmt.Fprintln(w, "This is a GET request")
 case http.MethodPost:
  fmt.Fprintln(w, "This is a POST request")
 default:
  http.Error(w, "Method not allowed", http.
StatusMethodNotAllowed)
 }
}
```

```
func main() {
 http.HandleFunc("/method", methodHandler)
 http.ListenAndServe(":8080", nil)
}
```

Here, the **/method** route handles different HTTP methods like GET and POST. The handler **methodHandler** uses **r.Method** to determine the request type. For unsupported methods, a **405 Method Not Allowed** error is returned.

URL path variables

This example demonstrates how to work with dynamic URL paths where part of the route, such as a user ID, changes based on the request. By extracting these path segments, the server can provide targeted responses, making it useful for resource-based APIs.

```
package main

import (
 "fmt"
 "net/http"
 "strings"
)
func dynamicHandler(w http.ResponseWriter, r *http.
Request) {
 id := strings.TrimPrefix(r.URL.Path, "/user/")
 if id == "" {
  http.Error(w, "User ID not provided", http.
StatusBadRequest)
  return
 }
 fmt.Fprintf(w, "User ID: %s", id)
}
func main() {
 http.HandleFunc("/user/", dynamicHandler)
 http.ListenAndServe(":8080", nil)
}
```

The **/user/{id}** route dynamically extracts the **{id}** part from the URL. The handler **dynamicHandler** uses **strings.TrimPrefix** to get the variable part of the path. It returns an error if no ID is provided.

Serving static files

Web applications often need to serve static assets like HTML, CSS, JavaScript, or images. This example illustrates how to use **http. FileServer** to create a route for serving files from a designated directory, a key feature for static websites or assets in dynamic web applications.

```
package main

import (
 «net/http»
)
func main() {
 fs := http.FileServer(http.Dir("./static"))
 http.Handle("/static/", http.StripPrefix("/static/", fs))

 http.ListenAndServe(":8080", nil)
}
```

This example serves static files from a directory named **static**. The **http.FileServer** function is used to create a handler for the files. The **http.StripPrefix** removes the **/static/** prefix from the requested URL to correctly map file paths.

Middleware and context in HTTP servers

Middleware is a way to wrap HTTP handlers to perform pre and post-processing of requests. Contexts allow us to pass request-scoped values, cancellation signals, and deadlines across API boundaries.

Implementing middleware

Middleware plays a crucial role in web development by enabling developers to add functionality to HTTP request/response cycles without modifying core handler logic. It acts as a layer of processing that can perform tasks such as logging, authentication, compression, or request modification before delegating to the final handler.

Middleware can be implemented by creating a function that takes an **http.Handler** and returns a new **http.Handler**. Refer to the following:

```go
package main

import (
    "fmt"
    "net/http"
)

func loggingMiddleware(next http.Handler) http.Handler {
    return http.HandlerFunc(func(w http.
ResponseWriter, r *http.Request) {
        fmt.Println("Request received:", r.URL.Path)
        next.ServeHTTP(w, r)
    })
}

func helloHandler(w http.ResponseWriter, r *http.
Request) {
    fmt.Fprintln(w, "Hello, World!")
}

func main() {
    hello := http.HandlerFunc(helloHandler)
    http.Handle("/hello", loggingMiddleware(hello))
    http.ListenAndServe(":8080", nil)
}
```

This code demonstrates how to implement and use middleware in a Go HTTP server. The middleware **loggingMiddleware** wraps an **http.Handler** and returns a new **http.Handler**. Inside the wrapper, it logs the requested URL path using **fmt. Println** before calling **next.ServeHTTP**, which passes control to the original handler.

The **helloHandler** is a simple HTTP handler that responds with **"Hello, World!"** when accessed. In the **main** function, **helloHandler** is converted to an **http.Handler** using **http. HandlerFunc** and passed to **loggingMiddleware**. The wrapped handler is then registered to the **/hello** route using **http.Handle**. The server is started on port 8080 using **http.ListenAndServe**.

When a client accesses **/hello**, the **loggingMiddleware** logs the request path (**/hello**), and then the request is passed to **helloHandler**, which generates the response.

Using context in HTTP requests

The **context** package in Go is a powerful tool for managing request-scoped data, timeouts, deadlines, and cancellation signals within HTTP handlers. By integrating contexts into web servers, developers can handle long-running operations gracefully, respond to client cancellations, and manage resources effectively. This section explores how to use context in HTTP requests to create more robust and responsive applications.

The following example highlights how contexts can be used to manage long-running operations:

```go
package main
import (
    "context"
    "fmt"
    "net/http"
    "time"
)
func helloHandler(w http.ResponseWriter, r *http.Request) {
    ctx := r.Context()
    select {
    case <-time.After(2 * time.Second):
        fmt.Fprintln(w, "Hello, World!")
    case <-ctx.Done():
        fmt.Fprintln(w, "Request cancelled")
    }
}
func main() {
    http.HandleFunc("/hello", helloHandler)
    http.ListenAndServe(":8080", nil)
}
```

This code demonstrates how to use contexts to manage HTTP request lifecycles. The **helloHandler** retrieves the context of the incoming request using **r.Context()**. Inside the handler, a **select** statement waits for either a 2-second delay or the cancellation of the request via the context.

- If the delay completes first, the handler responds with **"Hello, World!"**.

- If the request is canceled (e.g., if the client closes the connection), the `ctx.Done()` channel is triggered, and the handler responds with `"Request cancelled"`.

In the **main** function, the `/hello` route is registered using `http.HandleFunc`, and the server is started on port **8080** using `http.ListenAndServe`.

By listening to the `ctx.Done()` channel, the server can detect when a client has canceled the request and stop further processing, conserving resources and improving responsiveness.

Conclusion

In this chapter, we explored how to work with JSON data and build web applications using Go's net/http package. We covered encoding and decoding JSON, handling JSON in HTTP requests and responses, and building a simple web server. We also learned about routing, middleware, and using context in HTTP servers. With these skills, you are now equipped to create robust and scalable web applications in Go.

The next chapter covers Go's logging capabilities with the log and slog packages, alongside its testing framework for writing unit tests, running benchmarks, and debugging code.

References

- Go's Standard Library Documentation:

  - JSON: **https://pkg.go.dev/encoding/json**

  - HTTP: **https://pkg.go.dev/net/http**

- Go Blog: JSON and Go:

  - Official Go blog post explaining JSON encoding and decoding: **https://blog.golang.org/json-and-go**

CHAPTER 9

Logging and Testing

Introduction

In the world of software development, logging and testing are indispensable tools that ensure the reliability and maintainability of applications. Logging provides insights into the behavior of a program, helping developers diagnose issues and understand application flow. This is especially critical in real-world scenarios, such as debugging microservices in a distributed system, monitoring production systems for anomalies, and troubleshooting failures in cloud-based applications.

Testing, on the other hand, verifies that code behaves as expected, preventing bugs and regressions. In **continuous integration (CI)** pipelines, automated tests act as gatekeepers. Tests ensure new code changes do not break existing functionality.

In this chapter, we will explore the logging capabilities provided by Go, including the use of the log package and the newer slog package for structured logging. We will also delve into Go's testing framework, covering how to write unit tests, run benchmarks, and effectively debug your code.

Structure

This chapter covers the following topics:

- Using the log package

- Structured logging with slog
- Go's testing framework
- Benchmarking Go code

Objectives

This chapter will equip you to implement basic and structured logging in your Go applications using the **log** and **slog** packages, write unit tests to ensure code correctness, run **tests** to validate functionality, and use **benchmarks** to measure performance. With these skills, you will be well-prepared to maintain high-quality Go applications.

Using the log package

The Go standard library includes a built-in **log** package that provides basic logging capabilities. While it lacks advanced features like log levels, it is sufficient for simple logging needs. The **log** package allows you to output messages to standard output or a file, making it easy to track application behavior.

Basic logging

The log message prefixes the **log** date and time to the **log** message.

Here is a basic example of using the **log** package:

```go
package main

import (
    "log"
)

func main() {
    log.Println("Default logger: Application started")
}
```

The output of the program looks like this:

```
2024/12/17 08:57:43 Default logger: Application started
```

Adding flags for more information

The **log** package allows you to add flags to include additional information, such as timestamps with microseconds or file details:

```
log.SetFlags(log.LstdFlags | log.Lmicroseconds |
  log.Lshortfile)
log.Println("Logger with flags: Including timestamp and
file details")
```

In the code, we use the following flags:

- **LstdFlags**: Includes the date and time.
- **Lmicroseconds**: Adds microsecond precision to timestamps.
- **Lshortfile**: Includes the filename and line number of the log statement.

These flags change the output like this:

```
2024/12/17 08:57:43.327604 main.go:13: Logger with flags:
Including timestamp and file details
```

Using custom prefixes

Prefixes help categorize or identify the source or type of the log, which is especially useful in applications with multiple components or modules. The **log** package provides a convenient way to add custom prefixes to log messages when creating a logger.

To create a custom logger with a prefix, use the **log.New** function, as shown in the following example:

```
package main

import (
    "log"
    "os"
)

func main() {
    customLogger := log.New(os.Stdout, "[CUSTOM] ", log.
```

```
LstdFlags|log.Lmsgprefix)
    customLogger.Println("Logging with a custom prefix")
}
```

Here is a breakdown of the components:

- **os.Stdout**: Specifies the output destination for the logs, in this case, the console.

- **[CUSTOM]**: This is the prefix that gets added to every log message. You can customize this string to indicate the context of the log messages (e.g., `[DEBUG]`, `[ERROR]`, `[MODULE-X]`).

- **log.LstdFlags | log.Lmsgprefix**: Combines standard flags with the `Lmsgprefix` option, which ensures that the custom prefix is displayed before the log message.

When the above code is executed, the output will look like this:

`2024/12/17 08:57:43 [CUSTOM] Logging with a custom prefix`

Logging to a buffer

Logging to a buffer is useful for scenarios like testing or capturing logs in-memory without persisting them to a file.

```
package main

import (
    "bytes"
    "fmt"
    "log"
)

func main() {
    var buffer bytes.Buffer
    bufferLogger := log.New(&buffer, "[BUFFER] ", log.
LstdFlags)
    bufferLogger.
Println("This log is written to a buffer")
    fmt.Println(buffer.String())
}
```

Here, a logger is created with the buffer as its output, along with a **[BUFFER]** prefix and timestamp flags. A log message is written to the buffer using **bufferLogger.Println**. The contents of the buffer are then retrieved and printed to the standard log output using **buffer.String()**.

Here is the output of the program:

```
[BUFFER] 2024/12/17 08:57:43 This log is written to a
buffer
```

Logging to a file

Persisting logs to a file is crucial for long-term debugging and monitoring. It ensures that even if the application crashes or restarts, the logs remain accessible for post-mortem analysis or auditing purposes.

```
file, err := os.OpenFile("app.log", os.O_CREATE|os.O_
WRONLY|os.O_APPEND, 0666)
if err != nil {
    log.Fatal("Error opening log file:", err)
}
defer file.Close()
fileLogger := log.New(file, "[FILE] ", log.LstdFlags)
fileLogger.Println("This log is written to a file")
```

This code opens (or creates) a file named **app.log** in append mode with write-only access and appropriate permissions (**0666**). If the file cannot be opened, it logs the error and exits. Using **defer**, the file is closed when the function exits. A custom logger is created with **log.New**, configured to write logs to the file with a **[FILE]** prefix and timestamps using **log.LstdFlags**. Finally, a sample log message is written to the file using **fileLogger.Println**.

The log in the file **app.log** file looks like this:

```
[FILE] 2024/12/17 08:57:43 This log is written to a file
```

Structured logging with slog

Modern applications require structured logging to include context in key-value pairs. The **slog** package, introduced in **Go 1.21** is a powerful tool designed to simplify and enhance structured logging.

With **slog**, developers can log messages with associated metadata. It makes it easier to filter, search, and understand logs in complex systems. This structured approach is particularly useful in microservices, cloud-native applications, and production environments where logs are often aggregated and analyzed using tools like **Elasticsearch** or **Loki**.

While third-party loggers like **zap** and **logrus** have been popular choices for structured logging, **slog** offers a few advantages:

- **Standardized API**: As part of the Go standard library, **slog** ensures consistency and long-term support.

- **Performance**: slog is optimized for efficient structured logging, comparable to **zap**.

- **Customizable handlers**: It supports custom handlers for writing logs to various outputs, such as files, consoles, or external systems.

Although **zap** remains one of the fastest third-party loggers, and **logrus** is known for its ease of use, **slog** strikes a balance between performance, simplicity, and integration with the Go ecosystem. This makes **slog** a compelling choice for new Go projects.

JSON logging made easy

We can simply use slog by importing the **log/slog** package. **slog** provides a **NewJSONHandler** function to create a handler specifically designed for JSON output, as shown:

```
import (
  "log/slog"
  "os"
)

jsonHandler := slog.NewJSONHandler(os.
Stdout, nil) // Send logs to standard output
jsonLogger := slog.New(jsonHandler)
```

Then, create a logger instance using the **jsonHandler**. Now you can leverage various logging methods like **jsonLogger.Info** to log messages. Here is an example:

```
jsonLogger.Info("Structured log: Application started")
```

This will generate a JSON-formatted log entry containing the timestamp, level (**INFO**), and message.

```
{"time":"2024-12-19T23:17:50.123Z","level":"INFO","msg":"S
tructured log: Application started"}
```

Adding contextual information

Structured logging shines by allowing us to add contextual data to logs. This data can be anything relevant to the logged event, like module names, user IDs, or error codes. Use key-value pairs to include this context, as shown:

```
jsonLogger.Info("Structured log with context",
                "module", "main",
                "event", "startup",
                "user", "admin")
```

This outputs valuable insights into the context of the application startup:

```
{"time":"2024-12-19T23:17:50.123Z","le
vel":"INFO","msg":"Structured log with
context","module":"main","event":"startup","user":"admin"}
```

Including source information

Sometimes, pinpointing the source of a log message can be crucial for debugging. slog allows you to include the source file and line number in your logs using the **AddSource** option when creating the handler:

```
customSlogHandler := slog.NewJSONHandler(os.Stdout,
&slog.HandlerOptions{
  AddSource: true, // Include source file and line number
})
customSLogger := slog.New(customSlogHandler)
customSLogger.Info("Log with source information")
```

The console log will have the information about the file from where the log is generated. Here is how the log looks like:

```
{"time":"2024-12-17T09:02:45.873312291+05:30","level":"INF
O","source":{"function":"main.main","file":"/home/path_to_
code_directory/main.go","line":20},"msg":"Log with source
information"}
```

Filtering logs with levels

Real-world applications often generate a high volume of logs. slog provides different log levels (for example, **Debug**, **Info**, **Warn**, **Error**) to categorize messages based on their importance. You can configure a logger to filter logs based on their level:

```
customSlogHandler := slog.NewJSONHandler(os.Stdout, &slog.
HandlerOptions{
    Level: slog.LevelDebug,
})
customSLogger := slog.New(customSlogHandler)
customSLogger.Debug("Debugging information", "feature",
"new-logging", "status", "active")
customSLogger.Warn("This is a warning message", "module",
"logging", "severity", "high")
customSLogger.Error("Error encountered", "error",
"file-not-found", "retry", true)
```

Here, **slog.NewJSONHandler** creates a handler that outputs log messages in JSON format. **slog.HandlerOptions** sets the log level to Debug, ensuring logs with a severity of Debug and above are captured. Then, we create a logger, **customSLogger** that uses this custom JSON handler. Log messages include different log levels—**Debug**, **Warn**, and **Error**. The logs also use key-value pairs for additional context.

The output of this program looks like this:

```
{"time":"2024-12-17T09:02:45.873330845+05:30","level":
"DEBUG","msg":"Debugging information","feature":"new-
logging","status":"active"}
{"time":"2024-12-17T09:02:45.873334755+05:3
0","level":"WARN","msg":"This is a warning
message","module":"logging","severity":"high"}
```

{"time":"2024-12-17T09:02:45.873338219+05:30",
"level":"ERROR","msg":"Error encountered",
"error":"file-not-found","retry":true}

Go's testing framework

Testing is a cornerstone of reliable software development. It verifies that the code functions as intended, catching bugs early and preventing them from reaching production. Go provides a built-in testing framework through the **testing** package, streamlining the process of writing and executing tests. This section delves into Go's testing capabilities you can leverage in your projects.

Creating a test in Go involves defining a function whose name starts with **Test** and accepts a single argument of type ***testing.T**. This argument represents the test context and provides methods for reporting test results (pass/fail) and logging messages.

Here is an illustration testing a function that calculates product discounts:

```
package main

import "testing"

func TestCalculateDiscount(t *testing.T) {
  result := CalculateDiscount(100, 10)
// Apply 10% discount to $100
  expected := 90.0

  if result != expected {
    t.Errorf("CalculateDiscount(100, 10) = %.2f;
want %.2f", result, expected)
  }
}

func CalculateDiscount(price float64,
discountPercent float64) float64 {
  return price - (price * discountPercent / 100)
}
```

Writing unit tests

Unit tests focus on isolating and testing individual components of your application. By breaking down your codebase into testable units, you can ensure critical functions behave as expected.

Here is an example for a function validating user email formats:

```go
package main

import (
  "regexp"
  "testing"
)

func TestValidateEmail(t *testing.T) {
  tests := []struct {
    email    string
    expected bool
  }{
    {"user@example.com", true},
    {"invalid-email", false},
    {"", false},
    {"user@company.org", true},
  }

  for _, test := range tests {
    result := ValidateEmail(test.email)
    if result != test.expected {
      t.Errorf("ValidateEmail(%q) = %v; want %v", test.email, result, test.expected)
    }
  }
}

func ValidateEmail(email string) bool {
  // Simple regex pattern for email validation
  emailRegex := `^[a-zA-Z0-9._%+-]+@[a-zA-Z0-9.-]+\.[a-zA-Z]{2,}$`
  re := regexp.MustCompile(emailRegex)
  return re.MatchString(email)
}
```

This code demonstrates unit testing in Go by verifying the **ValidateEmail** function, which uses a regular expression to ensure the email follows a valid format. The test uses a table-driven approach, defining multiple test cases with inputs and expected outputs in a slice of structs. The test function iterates over these cases, calls **ValidateEmail**, and compares the result with the expected value. If there is a mismatch, **t.Errorf** logs a descriptive error message.

Here is the result of the test run:

```
=== RUN   TestValidateEmail
--- PASS: TestValidateEmail (0.00s)
PASS
```

Executing tests and understanding output

Running tests in Go is straightforward and integrated within the toolchain. We can use the **go test** command to execute all tests found in your package.

Here is how to run tests:

```
go test
```

When we run the validate email tests, we get the following output:

```
ok   command-line-arguments  0.001s
```

For a more comprehensive view, we can include the **-v** flag with **go test**:

```
go test -v
```

Now, the output is a little more elaborative:

```
=== RUN   TestValidateEmail
--- PASS: TestValidateEmail (0.00s)
PASS
ok        command-line-arguments      0.001s
```

Measuring test coverage

To measure how much of your code is covered by tests, we use the **-cover** flag:

```
go test -cover
```

This outputs the coverage percentage:

```
ok          command-line-arguments          0.002s     coverage:
85.7% of statements
```

For even more detailed coverage, you can generate an HTML report:

```
go test -coverprofile=coverage.out
go tool cover -html=coverage.out
```

Benchmarking Go code

Performance optimization is essential for resource-intensive operations. Go's testing package enables us to measure performance through benchmarks.

Here is an example benchmarking a function that calculates Fibonacci numbers:

```go
package main

import "testing"

func BenchmarkFibonacci(b *testing.B) {
  for i := 0; i < b.N; i++ {
    Fibonacci(20)
  }
}

func Fibonacci(n int) int {
  if n <= 1 {
    return n
  }
  return Fibonacci(n-1) + Fibonacci(n-2)
}
```

Benchmarking can be run with the following command:

```
$ go test -bench=.
```

The output of the program looks like this:

```
goos: linux
goarch: amd64
cpu: 11th Gen Intel(R) Core(TM) i5-11300H @ 3.10GHz
```

```
BenchmarkFibonacci-8            39064        30493 ns/op
PASS
ok      command-line-arguments    1.504s
```

Here is what the output means:

- The first three lines indicate the operating system (**goos**), architecture (**goarch**), and **CPU** details where the benchmark was executed.

- **BenchmarkFibonacci-8**: The name of the benchmark function (**BenchmarkFibonacci**) and the number of CPU threads (**8**) used during the benchmark.

- **39064**: The number of iterations (**b.N**) the benchmark ran. Go determines this value dynamically to achieve accurate results.

- **30493 ns/op**: The average time taken per iteration in nanoseconds (**ns/op**). Here, it takes approximately **30.5 microseconds** to compute Fibonacci(20).

Conclusion

In this chapter, we explored the essential aspects of logging and testing in Go. We learned how to use the log package for basic logging and the slog package for structured logging, providing valuable insights into application behavior. We also delved into Go's testing framework, covering how to write unit tests, run them, and interpret test output. Additionally, we explored benchmarking to measure the performance of specific code segments.

By mastering these techniques, you are now equipped to maintain high-quality Go applications with robust logging and testing practices. These practices also fit seamlessly into CI/CD pipelines, where automated testing ensures code quality, and structured logs simplify debugging.

The next chapter explores web development with Go, covering web servers, templating, form handling, framework integration, and authentication.

Join our book's Discord space

Join the book's Discord Workspace for Latest updates, Offers, Tech happenings around the world, New Release and Sessions with the Authors:

https://discord.bpbonline.com

CHAPTER 10

Go in Web Development

Introduction

Web development with Go has gained traction due to its simplicity, performance, and concurrency support. Unlike many other languages, Go offers a robust standard library with built-in packages like net/http for web servers and html/template for rendering dynamic content. This reduces the need for external dependencies. Go's strong typing and compile-time checks help catch errors early. The lightweight goroutines enable efficient handling of thousands of concurrent requests. Additionally, Go's cross-compilation support ensures seamless deployment across platforms.

In this chapter, we will explore how to build web applications using Go, covering essential concepts such as building a simple web server, templating, handling forms and user input, integrating with popular web frameworks, and implementing basic authentication and session management.

Structure

This chapter covers the following topics:

- Introduction to Go web development
- Building a basic web server with Go
- Using Go templates for dynamic content

- Handling forms and user input
- Integrating with web frameworks
- Basic authentication and session management

Objectives

By the end of this chapter, you will have a foundational understanding of web development in Go. You will learn how to set up a basic web server, use Go templates to render dynamic content, handle user input through forms, and integrate with popular web frameworks. Additionally, you will explore basic authentication and session management techniques to secure your web applications.

Introduction to Go web development

Go is designed to enable developers to rapidly develop scalable and secure web applications. Its standard library provides support for web development, like packages for handling HTTP requests, serving static files, and working with templates. Go's concurrency model makes it well-suited for handling multiple requests efficiently.

Here are some of the key benefits of using Go for web development:

- **Simplicity**: Go's syntax is clean and concise, making it easy to learn and write maintainable code.

- **Performance**: Go is a compiled language that produces efficient machine code. This makes web applications developed in Go fast and responsive.

- **Concurrency**: Go's built-in support for concurrency with goroutines and channels makes it ideal for building applications that handle multiple requests simultaneously.

- **Standard library**: Go's standard library provides a rich set of packages for web development.

Best practices for Go web development

Let us look at a few best practices that can help you build robust and production-ready web applications:

- **Security:**
  - Sanitize user inputs to prevent injection attacks.
  - Use HTTPS to encrypt data in transit.
  - Implement proper authentication and authorization mechanisms.

- **Scalability:**
  - Use goroutines efficiently for concurrent request handling.
  - Implement load balancing and caching to manage high traffic.
  - Optimize database queries and connection pooling.

- **Error handling:**
  - Always check for errors when working with I/O, databases, or external APIs.
  - Use structured logging to capture errors and application behavior.
  - Implement graceful shutdown using context cancellation to clean up resources.

Building a basic web server with Go

To start building web applications in Go, you need to set up a basic web server. Let us create a simple HTTP server that listens on a specified port and responds to requests:

```
package main

import (
  "fmt"
```

```go
    "net/http"
)

func homePage(w http.ResponseWriter, r *http.Request) {
    fmt.Fprintf(w, "Welcome to the Go Web Server!")
}

func main() {
    http.HandleFunc("/", homePage)
    fmt.Println("Server starting on port 8080...")
    http.ListenAndServe(":8080", nil)
}
```

In this example, we define a **homePage** function that writes a welcome message to the response writer. The **http.HandleFunc** function associates the root URL path (**"/"**) with the **homePage** handler. The **http.ListenAndServe** function starts the server on port **8080**.

Using Go templates for dynamic content

Go templates provide a powerful and flexible mechanism for generating HTML dynamically in web applications. They enable us to create web pages with variable data, making the applications more interactive and user-friendly.

Let us define a template **index.html** in the **templates** directory:

```html
<!DOCTYPE html>
<html lang="en">
    <head>
        <meta charset="UTF-8">
        <meta name="viewport" content=
"width=device-width, initial-scale=1.0">
        <title>{{ .Title }}</title>
    </head>
    <body>
        <h1>{{ .Message }}</h1>
    </body>
</html>
```

This template file contains placeholders for dynamic data within double curly braces **{{ }}**.

- **{{ .Title }}**: This placeholder will be replaced with the value of the **Title** key from the data map.

- **{{ .Message }}**: This placeholder will be replaced with the value of the **Message** key.

Here is the Go program that serves the dynamic content:

```go
package main

import (
  "html/template"
  "log"
  "net/http"
  "path"
)

// homePage is an HTTP handler that serves the homepage.
func homePage(w http.ResponseWriter, r *http.Request) {
  // Dynamic data to render
  data := map[string]string{
    "Title":   "Welcome",
    "Message": "Hello, Go Templates!",
  }

  fp := path.Join("templates", "index.html")
  tmpl, err := template.ParseFiles(fp)
  if err != nil {
    http.Error(w, err.Error(),
http.StatusInternalServerError)
    return
  }

  if err := tmpl.Execute(w, data); err != nil {
    http.Error(w, err.Error(),
http.StatusInternalServerError)
  }
}

func main() {
```

```
// Map the root URL path to the homePage handler
http.HandleFunc("/", homePage)

// Start the HTTP server on port 8080
log.Println("Server running on localhost:8080")
err := http.ListenAndServe(":8080", nil)
if err != nil {
  log.Fatal("ListenAndServe error:», err)
}
}
```

Here, the **homePage** function acts as the HTTP handler. A **data** map with dynamic content (**Title** and **Message**) is created. The template is stored in a **templates** directory for organization, and its file path is constructed using **path.Join**.

The **path.Join** function ensures that file paths are constructed correctly across different operating systems. While Windows uses backslashes (****) and **Unix-based** systems use forward slashes (**/**), **path.Join** handles these differences seamlessly. It concatenates path elements, removes redundant separators, and ensures a consistent format, avoiding common pitfalls when working with file paths.

The program ensures error handling, and returns appropriate HTTP error responses if the template fails to parse or render. The **main** function maps the root URL (**/**) to the **homePage** handler and starts an HTTP server on port **8080**. When accessed via a browser, the application dynamically generates an HTML page using the provided data as shown:

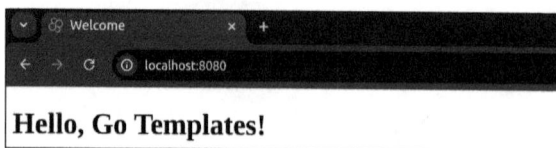

Figure 10.1: *Homepage with the title and the message*

Handling forms and user input

Handling forms and user input is a fundamental aspect of web development. It involves capturing data submitted by users through forms, validating it, and processing it for further use. This example demonstrates how to handle form submissions in Go, and user input processing upon submission.

This example consists of two files:

- **templates/index.html**: The HTML template containing the form.

- **main.go**: The Go program that handles form submissions and responses.

Here is the code of the template:

```
<!DOCTYPE html>
<html lang="en">
    <head>
        <meta charset="UTF-8">
        <meta name="viewport" content=
"width=device-width, initial-scale=1.0">
        <title>Submit Your Name</title>
    </head>
    <body>
        <h1>Enter Your Name</h1>
        <form action="/form" method="POST">
            <label for="name">Name:</label>
            <input type="text" id="name"
name="name" required>
            <button type="submit">Submit</button>
        </form>
    </body>
</html>
```

This HTML file provides a simple form:

- **action="/form"**: Specifies that the form data should be sent to the `/form` endpoint.

- **method="POST"**: Indicates the data will be sent via a **POST** request.

- **name="name"**: Sets the key for the form field, allowing the server to extract this value.

The code of the application is as follows:

```go
package main

import (
 "fmt"
 "net/http"
 "path"
 "html/template"
)

// indexHandler serves the HTML form for GET requests.
func indexHandler(w http.ResponseWriter, r *http.
Request) {
 fp := path.Join("templates", "index.html")
 tmpl, err := template.ParseFiles(fp)
 if err != nil {
  http.Error(w, err.Error(), http.
StatusInternalServerError)
  return
 }

 if err := tmpl.Execute(w, nil); err != nil {
  http.Error(w, err.Error(), http.
StatusInternalServerError)
 }
}

// formHandler processes POST requests for the form.
func formHandler(w http.ResponseWriter, r *http.Request) {
 if r.Method == http.MethodPost {
  // Retrieve the value of the "name" field from the form
  name := r.FormValue("name")
  if name == "" {
  // Handle empty input with a message
   http.Error(w, "Name field is required", http.
StatusBadRequest)
   return
  }
  // Respond with a personalized greeting
  fmt.Fprintf(w, "Hello, %s!", name)
  return
```

```
  }
  http.Error(w, "Invalid request method", http.
StatusMethodNotAllowed)
}

func main() {
  http.HandleFunc("/", indexHandler)

  // Map the /form route to the formHandler
  http.HandleFunc("/form", formHandler)

  // Start the HTTP server on port 8080
  fmt.Println("Server running on http://localhost:8080/
form")
  if err := http.ListenAndServe(":8080", nil); err != nil {
    fmt.Println("Error starting server:", err)
  }
}
```

In the main function, two handlers are registered for the root (/) and **/form** endpoints. The server is started on port **8080** and listens for incoming requests.

The **formHandler** function is the handler for the **/form** endpoint. It processes form submissions. First, we ensure only POST requests are processed. Then, **r.FormValue("name")** retrieves the value of the **name** field from the form. If the **name** field is empty, an **HTTP 400** error is returned. In the end, a personalized greeting (**"Hello, <name>!"**) is sent to the user.

Integrating with web frameworks

Go has several popular web frameworks that simplify web development by providing additional features and abstractions. Here are a few widely used frameworks of Golang:

- **Gin**: Gin is a lightweight and high-performance web framework that provides a simple API for building web applications. It is known for its speed and minimalism.

- **Beego**: Beego is a full-featured web framework that offers features like routing, ORM, and session management. It is suitable for building enterprise-level applications.

- **Echo**: It is another lightweight web framework that focuses on high performance and developer productivity.

- **Fiber**: Fiber is inspired by Express.js and built on top of Fasthttp, making it extremely fast and ideal for building modern web applications with minimal overhead.

- **Chi**: Chi is a lightweight, modular router for building HTTP services. It is well-suited for microservices and emphasizes composability with middleware chaining.

Here is an example of creating a basic web server using Gin:

```
package main

import (
 "github.com/gin-gonic/gin"
)

func main() {
 // Create a new Gin router with default middleware
 router := gin.Default()

 // Define a route for the root URL
 router.GET("/", func(ctx *gin.Context) {
  ctx.String(200, "Welcome to Gin!")
 })

 // Start the server on port 8080
 router.Run(":8080")
}
```

This example demonstrates a simple Gin web server that responds with a welcome message when the root URL (/) is accessed. The **gin.Default** function initializes a router with default middleware for logging and recovery, while the **router.GET** method sets up a handler for the **GET** request to the root endpoint. Finally, **router. Run** starts the server, listening on port **8080**.

Choosing the right web framework in Go depends on your project's needs, whether you prioritize speed, ease of development, or built-in features. The following table compares popular Go web frameworks to help you make an informed decision:

Gin	High	APIs, Microservices, high-traffic web apps	Large and active	Easy
Beego	Moderate	Full-stack web apps, enterprise apps	Moderate to large	Moderate
Echo	High	APIs, microservices, web apps	Large and active	Easy
Fiber	Very high	High-performance APIs, real-time apps	Growing and active	Easy
Chi	High	Microservices, API routers, composable HTTP services	Active and focused	Easy

Table 10.1: Web framework comparison

Basic authentication and session management

Authentication and session management are crucial components of web applications. Go provides libraries and techniques to implement these features securely. In this section, we will briefly cover these two topics.

To enhance the security of user authentication, consider using password hashing with **bcrypt** instead of storing plain-text passwords. Additionally, **JWT-based authentication** provides a stateless way to manage user sessions without relying on server-side storage. These approaches reduce the risk of credential leakage and improve the overall security posture of your web applications.

Basic authentication

Basic authentication involves verifying user credentials (username and password) before granting access to resources. Go's **http** package provides support for implementing basic authentication. Here is an example:

```
package main

import (
  "net/http"
```

```
)

func basicAuth(next http.HandlerFunc) http.HandlerFunc {
 return func(w http.ResponseWriter, r *http.Request) {
  username, password, ok := r.BasicAuth()
  if !ok || username != "admin" || password != "password" {
   w.Header().Set("WWW-Authenticate", `
Basic realm="Restricted"`)
   http.Error(w, "Unauthorized", http.StatusUnauthorized)
   return
  }
  next(w, r)
 }
}

func secretPage(w http.ResponseWriter, r *http.Request) {
 w.Write([]byte("Welcome to the secret page!"))
}

func main() {
 http.HandleFunc("/secret", basicAuth(secretPage))
 http.ListenAndServe(":8080", nil)
}
```

In the above code, a middleware function **basicAuth** wraps around a handler **secretPage** to enforce authentication. It extracts the username and password from the HTTP **Authorization** header using **r.BasicAuth()**. If the credentials do not match the predefined values, it responds with a **401 Unauthorized** status and prompts the client to provide valid credentials using the **WWW-Authenticate** header. If the authentication is successful, the request is passed to the wrapped handler (**secretPage**), which serves the protected content. The server listens on port **8080**, and accessing the **/secret** endpoint requires valid credentials.

Session management

Session management allows web applications to maintain user state across multiple requests. Sessions are typically stored server-side, with a session identifier sent to the client as a cookie.

Here is an example of basic session management using the **gorilla/sessions** package:

```go
package main

import (
 "fmt"
 "net/http"

 "github.com/gorilla/sessions"
)

var store = sessions.NewCookieStore([]byte("secret-key"))

func loginHandler(w http.ResponseWriter, r
*http.Request) {
 // Simulate login (replace with actual
authentication logic)
 username := r.FormValue("username")
 if username == "admin" {
  session, _ := store.Get(r, "session-id")
  // Set session values
  session.Values["username"] = username
  session.Save(r, w)
  fmt.Fprintln(w, "Login successful!")
  return
 }
 fmt.Fprintln(w, "Invalid username")
}

func logoutHandler(w http.ResponseWriter, r
*http.Request) {
 session, _ := store.Get(r, "session-id")
 // Remove session values
 session.Options.MaxAge = -1 // Mark session as expired
 session.Save(r, w)
 fmt.Fprintln(w, "Logged out successfully!")
}

func protectedHandler(w http.ResponseWriter, r *http.
Request) {
 session, _ := store.Get(r, "session-id")
 // Check if user is logged in
 if username, ok := session.Values["username"].
(string); ok {
```

```
  fmt.Fprintf(w, "Welcome, %s!", username)
  return
 }
 http.Error(w, "Unauthorized", http.StatusUnauthorized)
}

func main() {
 http.HandleFunc("/login", loginHandler)
 http.HandleFunc("/logout", logoutHandler)
 http.HandleFunc("/protected", protectedHandler)

 fmt.Println("Server running on http://localhost:8080")
 http.ListenAndServe(":8080", nil)
}
```

The above code sets up three endpoints: **/login**, **/logout**, and **/protected**. The **loginHandler** simulates user login by checking if the provided username matches **"admin"**. If valid, it creates a session, stores the username in the session, and sends a success response. The **logoutHandler** invalidates the session by setting its **MaxAge** to **-1**, effectively logging the user out. The **protectedHandler** checks for an active session and retrieves the username; if authenticated, it responds with a personalized message. Otherwise, it returns a **401 Unauthorized** error. The application uses cookie-based sessions with a secure key for storage, ensuring session data remains safe. The server runs on **http://localhost:8080**.

Conclusion

This chapter introduced us to web development with Go. It also covered essential concepts such as building a basic web server, using templates for dynamic content, handling forms and user input, and integrating with popular web frameworks. We also discussed topics like implementing basic authentication and session management. With these foundational skills, you are now equipped to build scalable and secure web applications using Go.

In the next chapter, we will explore Go's role in distributed systems. It will cover microservices, the context package, Kafka integration, and Redis-based distributed locks.

CHAPTER 11

Go in Distributed Systems

Introduction

In modern software development, distributed systems have become a cornerstone for building scalable and resilient applications. Go, with its simplicity and efficiency, is well-suited for developing such systems. This chapter delves into the use of Go in distributed systems, focusing on microservices, the context packages, and integrating with Apache Kafka using the Sarama library. We will also explore implementing distributed locks using Redis.

Structure

This chapter covers the following topics:

- Introduction to distributed systems and microservices
- Using the context package for request-scoped data
- Interaction with Kafka
- Distributed lock using Redis

Objectives

By the end of this chapter, you will understand how Go can be leveraged to build distributed systems. You will learn about microservices architecture and how to manage request-scoped data using the context package. You will learn to integrate Go applications with Apache Kafka using the Sarama library. Additionally, you will gain insights into implementing distributed locks using Redis.

Introduction to distributed systems and microservices

Distributed systems consist of multiple components located on different networked computers that communicate and coordinate their actions by passing messages. Microservices architecture is a variant of distributed systems where applications are structured as a collection of loosely coupled services. Each service is fine-grained, and the protocols are lightweight.

Go's concurrency model, efficient memory management, and a robust standard library make it an excellent choice for building microservices. Its lightweight goroutines enable scalable concurrent processing. The built-in gRPC support facilitates high-performance communication between services. Additionally, Go's ability to compile to a single binary simplifies deployment and improves portability.

Using the context package for request-scoped data

The context package in Go is essential for managing request-scoped data, cancellations, and deadlines. It allows for the propagation of request-scoped values and signals across API boundaries and goroutines.

Here is an example we will use context for timeout:

```
package main

import (
    «context»
    «fmt»
    «time"
)
```

```
func main() {
    ctx, cancel := context.WithTimeout(context.
Background(), 2*time.Second)
    defer cancel()

    select {
    case <-time.After(1 * time.Second):
        fmt.Println("Operation completed")
    case <-ctx.Done():
        fmt.Println("Operation timed out")
    }
}
```

This code demonstrates the use of **context.WithTimeout** function to handle timeouts for an operation.

A **context.WithTimeout** is created with a two-second timeout. This context will automatically cancel itself after two seconds. The **cancel** function is deferred to ensure the context is cleaned up properly, even if the operation completes before the timeout.

The **select** statement waits for one of two channels to send a signal:

- **time.After(1 * time.Second)**: Simulates an operation that takes 1 second to complete. If this case executes first, it prints **"Operation completed"**.

- **ctx.Done()**: This channel is closed when the context times out or is canceled. If this case executes, it prints **"Operation timed out"**.

Since the simulated operation takes 1 second and the context has a 2-second timeout, the **"Operation completed"** message is printed, as the operation finishes before the timeout occurs.

Interaction with Kafka

Apache Kafka is a distributed streaming platform that is widely used for building real-time data pipelines and streaming applications. It is designed to handle high-throughput, fault-tolerant, and scalable message processing.

Kafka is a powerful distributed messaging system often used in modern distributed architectures. In this section, we explore how to use the **Sarama** library to interact with Kafka. Sarama is a popular Go client library for Kafka, and it provides a rich set of APIs for producing and consuming messages.

We will walk you through a Kafka producer that sends messages (orders) and a Kafka consumer that processes these messages. The example revolves around a coffee shop, where customers place orders that are sent to Kafka and later consumed for processing.

Here is the code for a Kafka producer that sends customer orders to a Kafka topic:

```go
package main

import (
 "encoding/json"
 "log"

 "github.com/IBM/sarama"
)

// Order struct
type Order struct {
 CustomerName string `json:"customer_name"`
 CoffeeType   string `json:"coffee_type"`
}

func PushOrderToQueue(topic string, message []
byte) error {
 brokers := []string{"localhost:9092"}
 // Create connection
 producer, err := sarama.NewSyncProducer(brokers, nil)
 if err != nil {
  return err
 }

 defer producer.Close()

 // Create a new message
 msg := &sarama.ProducerMessage{
  Topic: topic,
```

```go
    Value: sarama.StringEncoder(message),
}

// Send message
partition, offset, err := producer.SendMessage(msg)
if err != nil {
    return err
}

log.Printf("Order is stored in topic(%s)/partition(%d)
/offset(%d)\n",
    topic,
    partition,
    offset)

return nil
}

func main() {
orders := []Order{
    {CustomerName: "Zorg Blaster", CoffeeType: "Espresso"},
    {CustomerName: "Nova Quasar", CoffeeType: "Latte"},
    {CustomerName: "Orion Vortex", CoffeeType: "Cappuccino"},
    {CustomerName: "Luna Starlight", CoffeeType: "Americano"},
    {CustomerName: "Echo Nebula", CoffeeType: "Mocha"},
}

for _, order := range orders {
    orderInBytes, _ := json.Marshal(order)
    PushOrderToQueue("coffee_orders", orderInBytes)
}
}
```

This code is responsible for orchestrating the process of sending coffee orders to Kafka. It defines an **Order** struct to represent each order. A connection is established with the Kafka broker using Sarama's SyncProducer API, and then the order is encoded as a JSON message. The encoded message is then sent to the **coffee_ orders** topic in Kafka. For each message, the producer logs the partition and offset where it is stored.

Here is the code for a Kafka consumer that processes the coffee orders:

```go
package main

import (
    "fmt"

    "github.com/IBM/sarama"
)

func main() {
    topic := "coffee_orders"

    // Create a new consumer and start it.
    config := sarama.NewConfig()
    config.Consumer.Return.Errors = true

    brokers := []string{"localhost:9092"}
    worker, err := sarama.NewConsumer(brokers, config)
    if err != nil {
        panic(err)
    }

    consumer, err := worker.ConsumePartition(topic,
0, sarama.OffsetOldest)
    if err != nil {
        panic(err)
    }

    defer worker.Close()

    fmt.Println("Consumer started ")

    // Run the consumer / worker.
    for {
        select {
        case err := <-consumer.Errors():
            fmt.Println(err)
        case msg := <-consumer.Messages():
            fmt.Printf("Received order: Topic(%s)
| Message(%s) \n", string(msg.Topic), string(msg.Value))
            order := string(msg.Value)
```

```
        fmt.Printf("Brewing coffee for order: %s\n",
order)
        }
    }
}
```

This code processes coffee orders by connecting to the Kafka broker and consuming messages from the **coffee_orders** topic. It continuously listens for new messages, retrieves them, and processes them. Here, it only prints the content of the order simulating coffee preparation.

Distributed lock with Redis

In distributed systems, ensuring data consistency and preventing race conditions are critical challenges. For example, imagine multiple instances of a service processing the same task concurrently, leading to duplicate processing or inconsistent state changes. Distributed locks coordinate access to shared resources across multiple nodes and ensure only one process can operate on a resource at a time.

Redis is an excellent choice for implementing distributed locks due to its simplicity, speed, and support for atomic operations. With its low-latency data store and support for operations like **SETNX** (set if not exists), it ensures that locks are acquired atomically. Redis also provides features like **time-to-live** (**TTL**) for locks, that prevents deadlocks by releasing locks automatically after a specified time if the process holding the lock fails.

Let us look at the following example:

```
package main

import (
  "context"
  "fmt"
  "time"

  "github.com/go-redis/redis/v9"
)
```

```go
func acquireLock(client *redis.
Client, lockKey string, timeout time.Duration) bool {
 ctx := context.Background()

 // Try to acquire the lock with SETNX command
(SET if Not eXists)
 lockAcquired, err := client.SetNX(ctx, lockKey,
"1", timeout).Result()
 if err != nil {
  fmt.Println("Error acquiring lock:", err)
  return false
 }

 return lockAcquired
}

func releaseLock(client *redis.Client, lockKey string) {
 ctx := context.Background()
 client.Del(ctx, lockKey)
}

func main() {
 // Create a Redis client.
 client := redis.NewClient(&redis.Options{
  Addr: "localhost:6379",
 })

 defer client.Close()

 // Define the lock key and lock timeout
 lockKey := "my_lock"
 lockTimeout := 20 * time.Second

 // Acquire the lock
 if acquireLock(client, lockKey, lockTimeout) {
  fmt.Println("Lock acquired successfully!")
  // Simulate some work with the lock
  time.Sleep(20 * time.Second)
  fmt.Println("Work done!")

  // Release the lock
  releaseLock(client, lockKey)
```

```
  fmt.Println("Lock released.")
 } else {
  fmt.Println("Failed to acquire lock. Resource is
already locked.")
 }
}
```

The above code shows a simple implementation of a distributed lock using Redis. The **acquireLock** function attempts to acquire a lock on a specified **lockKey** by using Redis' **SETNX** (set if not exists) command, ensuring that the key is only set if it does not already exist. If successful, the lock is set with a timeout to prevent indefinite locking in case of failures. The **releaseLock** function releases the lock by deleting the key from Redis. In the **main** function, a Redis client is initialized, and a lock key (**my_lock**) and timeout (20 seconds) are defined. The program attempts to acquire the lock, and if successful, simulates work for the duration of the lock before releasing it. If the lock cannot be acquired, it indicates that the resource is already locked. This approach ensures mutual exclusion for critical sections in distributed systems.

Conclusion

In this chapter, we explored how Go can be effectively used in distributed systems. We covered the basics of microservices architecture and how to manage request-scoped data using the context package. We also learned to integrate Go applications with Apache Kafka using the Sarama library. Finally, we explored implementing distributed locks using Redis. With these tools and techniques, you are well-equipped to build robust and scalable distributed systems in Go.

In the next chapter, we will cover generics in Go. We will learn the generics' syntax, type parameters, constraints, and creating reusable, type-safe functions and data structures.

Join our book's Discord space

Join the book's Discord Workspace for Latest updates, Offers, Tech happenings around the world, New Release and Sessions with the Authors:

https://discord.bpbonline.com

CHAPTER 12
Generics

Introduction

In this chapter, we will explore one of Go's most anticipated features—generics. Generics were introduced in Go 1.18. Generics enable us to write reusable and flexible code by making functions and data structures to work with any data type while maintaining type safety. This chapter provides a guide to the syntax and structure of generics, from simple type parameters to advanced constraints. You will learn how to create generic functions and types, and use constraints to restrict type parameters.

Structure

This chapter covers the following topics:

- Introduction to generics
- Generics syntax
- Generic functions
- Generic types

Objectives

By the end of this chapter, you will understand the fundamentals of generics in Go, their syntax, and how to implement generic functions and types. You will also learn to apply constraints to type parameters and appreciate how generics streamline your code by reducing redundancy.

Introduction to generics

Generics was a highly anticipated addition to Go. Generics significantly enhance the language's ability to write reusable and type-safe code that works with multiple data types. Before generics, developers often resorted to interfaces or code duplication. Both these approaches had drawbacks in terms of type safety and maintainability. Generics address these issues and lead to cleaner, more efficient code.

Generics have the following advantages over interfaces and duplicating code for different types:

- **Increased reusability and flexibility**: Functions and data structures can now be written once and used with various types.

- **Preserved type safety**: Generics provide compile-time type checking. Hence, there is no need for runtime type assertions and type-related errors prevention.

- **Reduced boilerplate**: Generics eliminate the need for writing repetitive code for different types, resulting in cleaner and concise code.

Generics syntax

Generics are implemented using type parameters, which are placeholders for actual types. These type parameters are defined within square brackets [ ] immediately after the function or type name.

Here is an example of a generic function in Go:

```
func PrintSlice[T any](slice []T) {
 for _, value := range slice {
  fmt.Println(value)
 }
}
```

This function is generic and accepts a slice of any type (**T**). It iterates over the slice and prints each element, regardless of its type.

Generic functions

Generic functions are a powerful feature in Go that lets us write a single function that can operate on values of different types without requiring modification. This significantly reduces code duplication and improves code maintainability.

A generic function uses type parameters as placeholders for actual types. These type parameters are declared within square brackets **[]** after the function name. When the function is called, the Go compiler infers the actual type based on the arguments provided.

Let us take a closer look at the example of finding the minimum value in a slice:

```
package main

import (
        "fmt"
        "golang.org/x/exp/constraints"
)

// Min returns the minimum value in a slice of
ordered elements.
// It returns the zero value of T if the slice is empty.
func Min[T constraints.Ordered](slice []T) T {
        if len(slice) == 0 {
                var zero T // Important: Return
the zero value
for empty slices
                return zero
        }

        min := slice[0]
        for _, v := range slice {
                if v < min {
                        min = v
```

```
                    }
            }
            return min
    }

    func main() {
            intSlice := []int{3, 1, 4, 1, 5, 9, 2, 6}
            floatSlice := []float64{3.14, 1.59, 2.65, 3.58}
            stringSlice := []
string{"apple", "banana", "cherry", "date"}

            minInt := Min(intSlice)
            minFloat := Min(floatSlice)
            minString := Min(stringSlice)

            fmt.Printf("Minimum int: %d\n", minInt)
            fmt.Printf("Minimum float: %f\n", minFloat)
            fmt.Printf("Minimum string: %s\n", minString)

            emptySlice := []int{}
            minEmpty := Min(emptySlice)
            fmt.
Printf("Minimum empty slice: %d (zero value)\n", minEmpty)
    }
```

In this code, **Min[T   constraints.Ordered](slice   []T)** declares a generic function **Min**. **T** is the type parameter that represents the type of the elements in the slice. **constraints. Ordered** specifies that **T** must be a type that supports ordered comparisons using operators like <, >, <=, and >=. The **constraints** package provides pre-defined constraints, which covers integer, floating-point, and string types.

In **Min** function, the **if   len(slice)   == 0** block is crucial. If the input slice is empty, there is no minimum value. In this case, the function returns the zero value of the type **T**. The core logic iterates through the slice, comparing each element **v** with the current minimum **min**. If **v** is less than **min**, **min** is updated.

In the main function, when we call **Min(intSlice)**, the compiler infers that **T** is **int**. Similarly, it infers **T** as **float64** for

Min(floatSlice) and string for **Min(stringSlice)**. This is a key benefit of generics—you do not have to explicitly specify the type parameter.

Generic types

Generics in Go are not limited to functions. They can also be applied to types, specifically **structs** and **interfaces**. This capability lets us create reusable data structures that operate on values of various types without requiring separate implementations for each type.

Generic structs

A generic struct is a struct where one or more fields are defined using type parameters. This allows the struct to hold values of different types while maintaining type safety.

Let us look at this implementation of generic stack:

```
package main

import "fmt"

// Stack is a generic stack data structure.
type Stack[T any] struct {
    elements []T
}

// Push adds an element to the top of the stack.
func (s *Stack[T]) Push(element T) {
    s.elements = append(s.elements, element)
}

// Pop removes and returns the top element from the stack.
// It returns a zero value of T and false if
the stack is empty.
func (s *Stack[T]) Pop() (T, bool) {
    if s.IsEmpty() {
        var zero T
        return zero, false // Return zero value and false
if stack is empty
    }
```

```go
    element := s.elements[len(s.elements)-1]
    s.elements = s.elements[:len(s.elements)-1]
    return element, true
}

// IsEmpty returns true if the stack is empty,
false otherwise.
func (s *Stack[T]) IsEmpty() bool {
    return len(s.elements) == 0
}

func main() {
    intStack := Stack[int]{}
    intStack.Push(1)
    intStack.Push(2)
    intStack.Push(3)

    val, ok := intStack.Pop()
    if ok {
        fmt.Println("Popped int:", val)
// Output: Popped int: 3
    }

    val, ok = intStack.Pop()
    if ok {
        fmt.Println("Popped int:", val)
// Output: Popped int: 2
    }

    stringStack := Stack[string]{}
    stringStack.Push("hello")
    stringStack.Push("world")

    strVal, ok := stringStack.Pop()
    if ok {
        fmt.Println("Popped string:", strVal)
// Output: Popped string: world
    }

    emptyStack := Stack[int]{}
    _, ok = emptyStack.Pop()
    if !ok {
```

```
        fmt.Println("Cannot pop from an empty stack")
// Output: Cannot pop from an empty stack
    }
}
```

In this implementation of generic stack data structure using generics (**T** any) to support any data type. The **Stack** type uses a slice to store elements and provides methods for common stack operations. The **Push** method adds an element to the top of the stack, and the **Pop** method removes and returns the top element. The **IsEmpty** method checks if the stack has no elements. The **main** function demonstrates its use with both **int** and **string** types. This approach highlights the flexibility and type safety of Go's generics for reusable data structures.

Generic interfaces

While less common than generic structs, you can also define generic interfaces. You can define interfaces that specify methods that operate on type parameters. This is particularly useful when working with more complex abstractions.

The following code shows how a generic interface can be implemented by a generic type:

```
package main

import "fmt"

// Container defines an interface for types that
can hold elements of a specific type.
type Container[T any] interface {
    Add(T)
    Get() (T, bool)
}

// MySlice implements the Container interface.
type MySlice[T any] []T

func (ms *MySlice[T]) Add(val T) {
    *ms = append(*ms, val)
}
```

```go
func (ms *MySlice[T]) Get() (T, bool) {
    if len(*ms) == 0 {
        var zero T
        return zero, false
    }
    val := (*ms)[0]
    *ms = (*ms)[1:]
    return val, true
}

func main() {
    var intContainer Container[int] = &MySlice[int]{}
    intContainer.Add(10)
    val, ok := intContainer.Get()
    if ok {
        fmt.Println(val) // Output: 10
    }

    var stringContainer Container[string] =
&MySlice[string]{}
    stringContainer.Add("Hello")
    strVal, ok := stringContainer.Get()
    if ok {
        fmt.Println(strVal) // Output: Hello
    }
}
```

This code uses a generic interface **Container[T any]** and a type
MySlice[T any] that implements it. The **Container** interface
defines two methods: **Add**, which adds an element of type **T** to
the container, and **Get**, which retrieves and removes the first
element. The **MySlice** type is a slice-based implementation of the
Container interface, with methods to append elements (**Add**) and
retrieve elements in a FIFO manner (**Get**).

In the **main** function, two containers are created—one for **int**
and one for **string**. Elements are added to the containers using
Add, and then retrieved using **Get**. The **MySlice** implementation
ensures type safety through Go's generics. For example, the
integer container retrieves the value **10**, and the string container
retrieves **"Hello"**.

Custom constraints

While the constraints package provides several useful pre-defined constraints like **constraints.Ordered**, you will often encounter situations where you need to define your own custom constraints to enforce specific type parameters. This allows you to tailor generic functions and types to your requirements.

Constraints are defined using interfaces. An interface defines a set of methods that a type must implement to satisfy the interface. When used as a constraint, the interface specifies the methods that a type parameter must have.

Type sets in interfaces provide a concise way to define constraints that allow a set of specific types. You can define a custom constraint like this:

```go
package main

import "fmt"

// Signed is a constraint that permits any
signed integer type.
type Signed interface {
    ~int | ~int8 | ~int16 | ~int32 | ~int64
}

// Abs returns the absolute value of x.
func Abs[T Signed](x T) T {
    if x < 0 {
        return -x
    }
    return x
}

func main() {
    fmt.Println(Abs(-5))       // Output: 5
    fmt.Println(Abs(int8(-10))) // Output: 10
    fmt.Println(Abs(int64(-15))) // Output: 15
}
```

In this code, the ~ symbol in the **type** set **~int | ~int8 | ~int16 | ~int32 | ~int64** means all types whose underlying type is int, int8, etc. This allows us to include named types based on these underlying types as well.

Conclusion

In this chapter, we explored how Go can be effectively used in distributed systems. We covered the basics of microservices architecture and how to manage request-scoped data using the context package. We also learned to integrate Go applications with Apache Kafka using the Sarama library. Finally, we explored implementing distributed locks using Redis. With these tools and techniques, you are well-equipped to build robust and scalable distributed systems in Go.

The following chapter covers securing Go applications using the crypto package, hashing, encryption, secure random generation, and authentication with JWT.

Join our book's Discord space

Join the book's Discord Workspace for Latest updates, Offers, Tech happenings around the world, New Release and Sessions with the Authors:

https://discord.bpbonline.com

CHAPTER 13

Go for Security and Cryptography

Introduction

Security is a crucial aspect of software development and Go provides robust tools to help developers secure their applications. In this chapter, we will explore how to secure your Go applications using the crypto package and best practices for writing secure Go code. We will cover the fundamentals of cryptography in Go, delve into hashing and encryption, learn how to generate secure random numbers, and understand how to handle user authentication and authorization with JWT.

Structure

This chapter covers the following topics:

- Introduction to cryptography in Go
- Hashing and encryption
- Generating secure random numbers
- Handling user authentication and authorization

Objectives

By the end of this chapter, you will have a solid understanding of how to implement cryptographic operations in Go. You will learn how to use the **crypto** package for hashing and encryption, generate secure random numbers, and implement authentication and authorization mechanisms in your Go applications.

Introduction to cryptography in Go

Cryptography is the practice of securing information by transforming it into a format that is unreadable to unauthorized users. Go's standard library provides a comprehensive set of cryptographic tools through its **crypto** package, which includes subpackages for various cryptographic operations such as hashing, encryption, and decryption.

Hashing and encryption

The **crypto** package offers several sub-packages for different cryptographic operations. The two commonly used ones are:

- **crypto/sha256** for hashing
- **crypto/aes** for encryption

Hashing with SHA-256

Hashing is a one-way cryptographic operation that transforms input data into a fixed-size string of characters, typically a hash code. The **crypto/sha256** package provides an implementation of the SHA-256 hashing algorithm.

Let us look at an example:

```
package main

import (
    "crypto/sha256"
    "fmt"
)

func main() {
    data := []byte("Hello, Go!")
    hash := sha256.Sum256(data)
    fmt.Printf("SHA-256 Hash: %x\n", hash)
}
```

Here, we use **sha256.Sum256** to compute the SHA-256 hash of the input data. The resulting hash is a fixed-size byte array:

```
SHA-256 Hash: d6ab13726c48971a34c0345e240bac7fc
19483491ec69c83d8148caf6ba3d130
```

Encryption with AES

Advanced Encryption Standard (AES) is a widely used symmetric encryption algorithm for securing data. The **crypto/aes** package provides an implementation of AES encryption.

Here is a simple example:

```go
package main

import (
    "crypto/aes"
    "crypto/cipher"
    "crypto/rand"
    "fmt"
    "io"
)

func encrypt(data []byte, key []byte) ([]byte, error) {
    block, err := aes.NewCipher(key)
    if err != nil {
        return nil, err
    }

    ciphertext := make([]byte, aes.BlockSize+len(data))
    iv := ciphertext[:aes.BlockSize]
    if _, err := io.ReadFull(rand.
Reader, iv); err != nil {
        return nil, err
    }

    stream := cipher.NewCFBEncrypter(block, iv)
    stream.XORKeyStream(ciphertext[aes.BlockSize:], data)

    return ciphertext, nil
}

func main() {
    key := []byte("a very very very very secret key")
// Must be 32 bytes
```

```go
    data := []byte("Hello, Go!")

    encryptedData, err := encrypt(data, key)
    if err != nil {
        fmt.Println("Error encrypting data:", err)
        return
    }

    fmt.Printf("Encrypted Data: %x\n", encryptedData)
}
```

In this example, we use the **crypto/aes** package to encrypt data using **AES** in **CFB** mode. The **encrypt** function takes the data and a 32-byte key as input and returns the encrypted data.

It is crucial to use a key with the correct length (32 bytes for AES-256). Shorter keys are less secure.

Generating secure random numbers

Generating secure random numbers is essential for cryptographic operations, such as generating keys or nonces. The **crypto/rand** package provides a way to generate cryptographically secure random numbers.

Here is an example code:

```go
package main

import (
    "crypto/rand"
    "fmt"
    "math/big"
)

func main() {
    n, err := rand.Int(rand.Reader, big.NewInt(100))
    if err != nil {
        fmt.Println("Error generating random number:", err)
        return
    }

    fmt.Printf("Secure Random Number: %d\n", n)
}
```

In this example, we use the **rand.Int** function from the **crypto/ rand** package to generate a secure random number between 0 and 99.

Handling user authentication and authorization

Authentication and authorization are critical components of securing web applications. Authentication verifies the identity of a user, while authorization determines what resources a user can access.

Implementing authentication

Authentication is the process of verifying a user's identity. In Go, you have several options for implementing authentication, each with its own advantages and considerations. This includes session-based authentication, API keys, OAuth, and **JSON Web Tokens (JWT)**.

JWTs are a popular choice for stateless authentication. They are compact, self-contained tokens containing information about the user (called claims) and a signature to ensure integrity. This allows the server to verify the user's identity without needing to maintain session state.

We will use the **github.com/golang-jwt/jwt/v5** package for handling JWT. This package can be Installed by running the following command in your project directory:

```
go get github.com/golang-jwt/jwt/v5
```

Here is a simple example of using JWT for authentication:

```
package main

import (
 "fmt"
 "net/http"
 "strings"
 "time"

 "github.com/golang-jwt/jwt/v5"
```

```go
)
var secretKey = []byte("your-secret-key")
func generateJWT(username string) (string, error) {
 // Create a new token object with claims
 token := jwt.NewWithClaims(jwt.SigningMethodHS256, jwt.
MapClaims{
   "username": username,
   "exp":       time.Now().Add(time.Hour * 24).
Unix(), // Expires in 24 hours
 })

 // Sign the token with the secret key
 tokenString, err := token.SignedString(secretKey)
 if err != nil {
  return "", err
 }

 return tokenString, nil
}
func validateJWT(tokenString string) (string, error) {
 // Parse the token
 token, err := jwt.Parse(tokenString, func(token *jwt.
Token) (interface{}, error) {
  // Ensure the signing method is as expected
  if _, ok := token.Method.(*jwt.SigningMethodHMAC); !ok {
   return nil, fmt.Errorf("unexpected signing method")
  }
  return secretKey, nil
 })

 if err != nil {
  return "", err
 }

 // Extract and verify claims
 if claims, ok := token.Claims.(jwt.
MapClaims); ok && token.Valid {
  username := claims["username"].(string)
  return username, nil
 }

 return "", fmt.Errorf("invalid token")
}
func loginHandler(w http.ResponseWriter, r *http.
```

```
Request) {
 if r.Method != http.MethodPost {
  http.Error(w, "only POST method is allowed", http.
StatusMethodNotAllowed)
  return
 }

 err := r.ParseForm()
 if err != nil {
  http.Error(w, "invalid form data", http.
StatusBadRequest)
  return
 }

 username := r.FormValue("username")
 password := r.FormValue("password")

 if username != "exampleUser" || password !=
 "password123" {
  http.Error(w, "invalid username or password", http.
StatusUnauthorized)
  return
 }

 token, err := generateJWT(username)
 if err != nil {
  http.Error(w, "failed to generate token", http.
StatusInternalServerError)
  return
 }

 w.Header().Set("Content-Type", "application/json")
 w.WriteHeader(http.StatusOK)
 fmt.Fprintf(w, `{"token": "%s"}`, token)
}
func secureHandler(w http.ResponseWriter, r *http.
Request) {
 authHeader := r.Header.Get("Authorization")
 if authHeader == "" {
  http.Error(w, "missing token", http.StatusUnauthorized)
  return
 }

 // Extract token from the "Bearer <token>" format
 tokenString := strings.TrimPrefix(authHeader, "Bearer ")
```

```
username, err := validateJWT(tokenString)
if err != nil {
  http.Error(w, "invalid token", http.StatusUnauthorized)
  return
}

fmt.Fprintf(w, "Welcome, %s!", username)
}
func main() {
  http.HandleFunc("/login", loginHandler)
  http.HandleFunc("/secure", secureHandler)
  http.ListenAndServe(":8080", nil)
}
```

In this code, we implemented JWT authentication by creating a simple HTTP server with two endpoints:

- **/login**: This endpoint allows users to authenticate and receive a JWT.

- **/secure**: A protected endpoint accessible only to users with a valid JWT.

The core of our implementation revolves around two functions:

- **generateJWT**: This function creates and signs a JWT for a given username. The token includes user-specific claims (like username) and metadata such as the expiration time. A new JWT token is created using the **jwt.NewWithClaims** function. The token is signed using the HS256 method, which is **Hash-based Message Authentication Code (HMAC)** algorithm. This ensures the token is secure and tamper-proof. The second argument to the function **jwt.NewWithClaims** is claims. Claims are pieces of information encoded in the token. In our case, it is the username and token's expiration time.

- **validateJWT**: This function validates the token and extracts the username from it. Its primary purpose is to parse a provided JWT token string, validate its integrity, and extract meaningful claims (**username**) from it. The function begins by using the **jwt.Parse** method, which requires a token string and a **callback** function to validate the token's signing method and provide the secret key for verification. Inside the **callback**, the signing method is checked to confirm it is an HMAC-based method (such as **HS256**), ensuring the token's expected security. If the token is invalid or parsing fails, the function returns an error. Once the token is successfully parsed, the claims within the token are accessed and verified for validity. If the token is valid and the claims are properly formatted, the username is extracted from the claims and returned. Otherwise, an error is returned, indicating that the token is invalid. This function is central to the application's security, as it ensures that only authorized requests with valid tokens can access protected resources.

The **loginHandler** function authenticates users and generates a JWT upon successful authentication. For simplicity, we use hardcoded credentials in this example. In a real application, you would validate the credentials against a database or an external authentication service.

The **secureHandler** function handles **/secure** route which is a protected resource. It validates the JWT passed in the Authorization header and grants access only if the token is valid.

We can use curl or Postman to test the **/login** endpoint. To send a POST request with the following parameters we can send the following command:

```
curl -X POST http://localhost:8080/login \
    -d "username=exampleUser" \
    -d "password=password123"
```

The expected response looks like this:

```
{"token": "<JWT_TOKEN>"}
```

Replace **<JWT_TOKEN>** with the token from the **/login** response and send a **GET** request to the **/secure** endpoint:

```
curl -X GET http://localhost:8080/secure \
    -H "Authorization: Bearer <JWT_TOKEN>"
```

If the correct token is passed in the header, the successful response looks like this:

```
Welcome, exampleUser!
```

Implementing authorization

While authentication answers **"Who are you?"**, authorization answers **"What can you do?"**. It is the process of determining what actions or resources the authenticated user is allowed to access.

Authorization can be implemented using **role-based access control (RBAC)** or **attribute-based access control (ABAC)**. As we have seen in the authentication example, JWT uses claims to create the token. For authorization, we can include roles, permissions, or access levels in claims. Here is an example of the claim:

```
{
  "username": "space_ranger",
  "role": "admin",
  "permissions": ["read", "write"]
}
```

When the JWT token is received with the request, the server checks these claims to decide if the user can perform a specific action or access a resource.

Conclusion

We explored the essential techniques for securing Go applications. We covered the basics of cryptography in Go, including hashing and encryption using the crypto package. We learned how to generate secure random numbers and implement user authentication and authorization using JWT. With these practices, you can build applications that protect sensitive data and ensure that only authorized users have access to resources.

Index